Praise for *Dare to Empower – Now*

"In *Dare to Empower–Now*, Maynor Morales puts, as we say in Spanish, 'his finger in the wound.' The key challenge for today's Hispanic leaders is to risk the empowerment of their best young followers. As a university president who is close to the new generation, I can promise that those who answer this call will be well rewarded!"

—Joseph Castleberry, Ed.D.
President Northwest University
and author of *The New Pilgrims: How Immigrants are Renewing America's Faith and Values*

"Dr. Maynor Morales has a passion for preparing clergy and lay leaders for the Emerging Hispanic Generation of Christians. He draws upon a wealth of multicultural, multilingual, and multinational pastoral experience in developing and empowering Hispanic leaders. Dr. Morales integrates biblical principles, contextual awareness, and practical guidelines for ministerial training. He is especially adept in focusing upon discipleship, mentoring, and spiritual formation for intergenerational and immigrational outreach. I highly recommend Morales's book for preparing leaders in Hispanic communities in ways that are biblically sound, culturally sensitive, and ministerially effective."

—Don Thorsen, Ph.D.
Professor of Theology, Azusa Pacific University Seminary

"This is a fine contribution to the emerging voice of Latino Pentecostal thinking. Dr. Morales combines a Pentecostal joy in scripture with a clear need to develop Pentecostal leadership in the Church and World."

—Rev. Isaac J. Canales, Ph.D.
The Mission Eben-Ezer Family Church.
Former President of Latin American Bible Institute and
Department and Assistant Professor, Fuller Theological Seminary

"As the Latino Protestant community continues to grow, it needs a new generation of leaders that can respond to the challenges of guiding a new generation of Latino believers to be faithful followers of Jesus Christ. Dr. Maynor Morales invites you to look at the work of one of the district's largest Latino Protestant denomination in the U.S., the Assemblies of God, as it addresses this challenge. His work provides important insights into their experience that can be used by anyone who is involved in this very important task."

—Juan Francisco Martínez, Ph.D.
Vice President for Diversity and International Ministries
Fuller Theological Seminary

"I am pleased to recognize the literary work of my dear friend Maynor Morales. A work from the heart of a knowledgeable and caring pastor, it explains the biblical guidelines for training a new generation of young people in our Hispanic churches: A generation that daily confronts false doctrines and seducing spirits that seek to divert them from God's standards. The contents of this book have enough doctrinal essence and biblical arguments to form the character and values of this generation and promote the development of our faith. My sincere congratulations to Dr. Maynor Morales for an excellent contribution. Congratulations champion."

—Presbyter Abel Flores Acevedo
General Superintendent of the Assemblies of God in Mexico

DARE TO EMPOWER - NOW

Developing Leaders in the Emerging Hispanic Generation

By

Dr. Maynor Morales

Dedication

To my wife, Evie; to my daughters, Krystal and Tiffany (who are part of the Emerging Hispanic Generation); to the memory of my parents, Matias and Silveria Morales; and most of all to the leader of leaders, Jesus Christ.

Contents

Acknowledgments. xi
Foreword. xiii
Introduction. xvii

Part A. THE HISPANIC CONTEXT

Chapter 1:   Background. 29
Chapter 2:   Challenges. 42

Part B. THE BIBLE AND EMERGING LEADERSHIP

Chapter 3:   Old Testament 55
Chapter 4:   New Testament 70

Part C. CASE STUDY: THE ASSEMBLIES OF GOD

Chapter 5:   Pentecostal Development in the
              United States. 89
Chapter 6:   Northern Pacific Latin American
              District Formation. 103

Part D. APPROACHES TO LEADERSHIP DEVELOPMENT

Chapter 7:   Leadership Development 121
Chapter 8:   Spiritual Formation 126
Chapter 9:   Discipleship. 150
Chapter 10:   Intergenerational Outreach 179
Chapter 11:   Mentoring 206

Conclusion 219
Notes 223
About the Author. 235

Acknowledgments

E vie, you are the love of my life. The encouragement, support and patience that you have provided to me during all my years of study is of immeasurable value. Thank you also to Krystal and Tiffany, my two beautiful daughters, for putting up with Dad and never complaining once about the long hours of study and research; always willing to sacrifice quality time that I could have spent with you. I am grateful to my father Matias and my mother Silveria, whose leadership legacy has encouraged me to pursue excellence in ministry.

I would also like to extend thanks to my brothers and sisters. Thank you, Mizrrahim, for giving me the opportunity to exercise and develop leadership skills as your associate pastor. Thank you Josue, my brother and friend, who alongside my relatives and friends, pushed me and encouraged me every day with the question, "Have you finished the chapter yet?" Adonias, Rene, Reyna, and Marina, I'm so grateful for your love and support.

Mentors are crucial for leadership development. Dr. Jesse Miranda, thank you for mentoring me and for being instrumental in my biblical studies at Azusa Pacific University. Dr. Enrique Zone, thank you for being my mentor during my Doctor of Ministry project at Azusa Pacific University. Dr. Don Thorsen, thank you for believing in me and motivating me to write this book.

To the wonderful church, New Dawn/Nuevo Amanecer, where I served as pastor for over fifteen years–thank you for your prayers, patience, and support during my doctorate journey. Thanks also to the executives of the Northern Pacific Latin American District for your vital information and support.

Finally, I would like to extend special thanks to my editors: my wife, Evie; my daughter Krystal; Irene Cruz; Janice Baskin; and Sally Casey.

Foreword

This book is about the call for the much-needed development of a future generation of young leaders and the organizational strategies to serve them. As I read through it, I was reminded of my experience at the age of eight. After a Sunday evening service, I sat on the church bench waiting for my mother to finish praying at the altar. Finally, she came and sat by my side, put her arms around me and whispered, "When you grow to be a man, I want you to be an educated man." Not knowing all that implied, I replied, "Yes mama!" Then she pointed to a young man fervently praying at the altar and said, "That is an educated man!" Jose Martinez was the youth leader of the church, a soloist in the radio program, and a deacon. He was also the only person I knew that had more than a high school diploma. He also had two college degrees and was a professor of engineering at the University of New Mexico. The image that was etched in me was a man with "a heart on fire and a mind ablaze."

Dare to Empower–Now reminds us not to forget the blessed experience of being converted to Christ, but it is also a plea to move forward toward intentional, relational, relevant and experiential discipleship and leadership. As a young convert I had elders and mentors who taught me that I was being called to a spiritual life–that quest for God that relies on the eye of the heart. But I was also taught that my response to that call was the development and the quest for knowledge: the eye of the mind. I have been forced to find ways for my eyes to work together to find a common focus for my spirit-seeking heart and my knowledge-seeking mind that embraces reality in all its amazing dimensions.

It is ardent passion and acute knowledge for the integration of a heart on fire and a mind ablaze that creates a bifocal vision and "double" listening: for service and ministry. It is a calling that lies in the intersection of the church, the campus and the community to all future generations. Herein lies the hope to foster a true and biblical discipleship for the much-needed revival of the Church and for the common good of the community.

I witnessed Maynor's leadership when he was young. I had the privilege of knowing the Morales family soon after they came from Guatemala. Maynor's father had already been an outstanding leader in his country. I got to know the family well and had the honor of performing the marriage ceremony of Maynor and his wife, Evie, and officiating at their twenty-fifth anniversary. I also witnessed Maynor's leadership abilities when I had him as a student and while I continued to mentor him. We have remained friends and he continues to be a successful leader.

Pastor Morales offers constructive advice and plans to help move Hispanic denominations toward the future. We don't know the future yet, only the past and present. One thing we do know is that the new generation will remain in the church not only because it preaches the truth but also because it makes the truth relevant to its culture and needs. The same is true of all Christians, the church, the district and all organizations. The means by which we bring the past, the present and the future together in our thinking and living is vital. Two great challenges are dealt with here. The tension between the 'then' (past), and the 'now' (present). Secondly, there is tension between the 'now' (present) and the 'not yet' (future). In all things and in all times, may God be glorified! One organizational legend to remember: Sow an action and you will reap a habit; sow a habit and reap a character; but sow a character and you will reap a destiny for the Church.

**—Dr. Jesse Miranda,
Executive Presbyter of the General Council of the
Assemblies of God, President of the Jesse Miranda Center
for Hispanic Leadership.**

Introduction

The year was 1962, and it was a beautiful morning in Guatemala City. A pastoral family of nine, with five sons and two daughters, was seated at the family table eating their breakfast, and the children were about to leave for school. Suddenly, there was a knock at the front door of the parsonage. Without hesitation, the smallest child of the family took off running through a long dirt hallway, which led to the front door.

"Who is it?" asked the little boy.

"It is me, Brother Juan."

"What is it that you want?"

"I need to talk to the senior pastor," was Juan's response, and then he began to elaborate on the reason for his request, "You see, I have a problem that requires the pastor's counsel as soon as possible."

The pastor's son opened the door, "I'm the senior pastor—you can share your problems with me." "But you are only five years old!" Juan responded playfully, "Furthermore, you are not Pastor Matias and I can't share my problem with you." The conversation that ensued was nothing short of that of a pastor's son emulating his father. The little child proudly raised his voice and articulated the following words: "My name is Matias, and this name happens to be the senior pastor's name, and so for your information,

I am the pastor. Furthermore, what you really need to do is to go straight to the church, kneel down before the altar, and begin to pray. I will lay hands on you. I know that after my prayer you will experience God's help."

By the time the senior pastor (the boy's father) arrived at the church, Brother Juan was already prayed for, felt at ease, and was ready to speak with the real senior pastor. This true and entertaining story is one that I will never forget. My father, Matias Morales, was the senior pastor of the aforementioned church, named Iglesia El Sinai. My late father, who died at the age of ninety five, was an active pastor whose passion for the Lord and for leadership flowed through his veins, and was engraved on his heart and soul. One can still remember his love and passion for leadership development, especially through the messages he delivered in the church he founded thirty three years ago in Harbor City, California.

It has been fifty-three years since the conversation in Guatemala City between the little boy and Brother Juan. The little five-year-old child who answered the door was me, and I am blessed to follow in my father's footsteps. I was the senior pastor of a church in Fremont, California, called New Dawn Worship Center/Centro de Adoración Nuevo Amanecer for over fifteen years. The church belongs to the Assemblies of God, which happens to be the same denomination of the church my father once pastored in Guatemala. Today, my two daughters are the ones in leadership training, and just as I did, they answer our door when members of the mission church we are currently planting request my assistance in spiritual matters.

My father has been my mentor, but more so he is one of the most influential people in my leadership development journey. I am not the only family member who can testify to my father's leadership development legacy. All seven of his sons and daughters who sat around the breakfast table that beautiful morning, fifty-three years ago, are now currently serving as leaders in their respective churches. Our ministerial legacy dates back to the early 1930s. We are the third generation of ministers within the Assemblies of God. The first and second generations of pastors and leaders within our family were raised in Guatemala. My grandfather, my father's uncle, and my father were amongst the first Assemblies of God's credentialed pastors in their country.

A very well-respected educator by the name of Virgilio A. Arceyuz wrote a book that compiles and narrates the history of the gospel in Guatemala. In his book, *Historia de La Iglesia Evangélica en Guatemala* (History of The Evangelical Church in Guatemala), he wrote a chapter on the birth of the Assemblies of God in Guatemala. In this chapter, Arceyuz records the first Assemblies of God Conference as well as the first ordained ministers:

> De esa manera, en Atescatempa, del 31 de diciembre de 1937 al 2 de enero de 1938, se celebró la primera Conferencia Anual de las Asambleas de Dios en Guatemala...En esa ocasión también se ordenó a los primeros pastores de las Asambleas de Dios en Guatemala, siendo ellos los hermanos Gerardo Ortiz, Toribio Ramírez, Lorenzo Morales, Félix Carias, Julián Morales...[1]

> (In that manner, in Atescatempa, from December 31, 1937 to January 2, 1938, the first Annual Conference of the Assemblies of God in Guatemala was celebrated...In that occasion, the first pastors of the Assemblies of God were ordained. The names of those ordained were: Brother Gerardo Ortiz, Toribio Ramirez, Lorenzo Morales, Felix Carias, Julian Morales...)

Lorenzo Morales was my grandfather and Julian Morales was my grandfather's brother. This book, alongside with many other documents, serves as a testament to the Morales's early involvement in ministry. During the 1940s the Rev. Juan L. Franklin (an Assemblies of God missionary to Guatemala) made an extensive missionary journey to towns along the Pacific coastline of Central America. In one of the towns he visited, Las Lisas, a group of people gave their hearts to the Lord. During this missionary journey, Juan Franklin placed my father, Matias Morales, as the pastor of this new mission.[2] Clearly, our family's Christian leadership development journey is not only blessed, but is one that has in mind the emerging generation.

I have taken the liberty of narrating these stories, not with the intention of boasting about our ministerial lineage, but rather to state the following point: **Christian leadership development works**. It works in all places, cultures, and generations, and in all Christian denominations. When the right strategies are embraced and implemented, and when the older generation of leaders gets involved, then in due course the end result will be a bountiful harvest of a new generation of leaders.

This Hispanic leadership book aims to develop a plan that will reap a healthy harvest of Christian leadership amongst the Emerging Hispanic Generation (E.H.G.) within our Hispanic denominations. Although this book targets the Christian emerging generation, one cannot deny the fact that the training of both clergy and lay leaders is especially crucial to the success of Hispanic Christianity and U.S. Christianity in general.

The Hispanic population in the United States is growing by the millions. At the present time, this group is the nation's largest and fastest growing minority group. According to the data from the 2010 U.S. census, the Hispanic population had increased by 35.3 million since the year 2000. In 2010, 50.5 million of the 308.7 million people residing in the United States, or 16 percent, were of Hispanic origin. Hispanics were responsible for more than half of the U.S. population growth during that decade.[3] According to the most recent U.S. Census Bureau projections, the Hispanic will grow by 86 percent between 2015 and 2050. By 2060, the Hispanic population will reach 119 million.[4] Another statistic that is worth mentioning is the one that shows Hispanics as the largest minority group. Hispanics will comprise 24 percent of the population (18 percent now).[5] Nearly one of every four people will be Hispanic.

If these projections prove to be accurate, we have in front of us a blessing as well as an enormous task. On one hand, every Hispanic denomination has the tremendous potential of harvesting thousands of E.H.G. leaders that could lead our churches toward a powerful and spiritual awakening among Hispanics. On the other hand, if the next generation of Hispanics is not mentored, trained, or discipled, we may experience a dreadful loss of leadership amongst Hispanic churches, resulting in a leadership setback.

To leave this problem unresolved is not the answer. To sweep it under the leadership carpet would be a denial of the task in front of us. The prevalent need for leadership development for the E.H.G. is imminent among our Hispanic churches. As we are now in the second decade of the twenty-first century, we find ourselves in desperate need of both pastors and lay leaders to partner and work together in this endeavor. What then should the answer to this problem be? What ought to be the role of the present generation of Hispanic leaders towards developing leadership within the E.H.G.? How can we ensure a harvest of Hispanic leaders that will serve the next generation? Furthermore, although we currently have Hispanic leaders that have influenced and produced new leaders for this generation through their service in their respective areas of ministry, there is still a need to develop a strategy that will ensure more Hispanic Leadership for the emerging generation.

This book outlines Christian leadership development approaches that may be an aid to the paramount task in front of us; moreover, it offers a practical method that could assist with the implementation of a Hispanic leadership development program. This program will include: (a) spiritual formation, (b) discipleship, (c) intergenerational outreach, (d) a mentoring ministry, and (e) a proposal for a Hispanic center for Hispanic leadership development. I understand the complexity of this endeavor. Part of the complexity is due to the current shortage of emerging generation leaders and ministers within our churches. There are millions of Hispanics within our states who are in need of the gospel of Jesus Christ. In order to accomplish this task, we need the help of the E.H.G. within our churches and Hispanic denominations. Understanding the great task before us, I am hopeful that this book will inspire more people to embark on the much needed task of publishing more articles and books related to this important and vital topic.

The intent of this book is not to ignore the unsurpassable work of our previous leadership and mentors. I am not trying to re-invent the leadership wheel, but rather to contribute new methods and ideas that can adequately address the generational changes that exist not only within our individual congregations, but perhaps in every Hispanic denomination. Thomas Jefferson, in regard to methods and principles, couldn't have phrased it better when he said, "In matters of style, swim with the current; in matters of principle, stand like a rock."[6] With the help of our Hispanic Christian leadership and with the guidance of the Holy Spirit, I am hopeful that this century will yield its greatest harvest of E.H.G. leaders amongst our beloved Hispanic denominations.

This book contains four main parts. Part A, The Hispanic Context, is an overview of Hispanic context within the United States. I give specific attention to the demographic analysis which shows the tremendous Hispanic growth within the United States, and the socioeconomic factors affecting the Hispanics. Distinct emphasis will be given to the dynamics, conflicts, and challenges between the first generation and the emerging generation of Hispanics within their respective settings.

Part B, The Bible and Emerging Leadership, explains the biblical context of the need for Christian leadership development for the E.H.G. First, we will examine the biblical leadership development found in the Old Testament. Second, we will explore the New Testament Leadership development introduced by Jesus Christ and later followed by His disciples. Next, we will study the role of the Holy Spirit in the biblical emerging generation. Finally, the biblical principles found in the scriptures will serve as the foundation for an effective Hispanic Christian leadership development program.

Part C, Case Study: The Assemblies of God, is a case study of a Hispanic district within the Assemblies of God. This Hispanic district is part of a Pentecostal denomination that has been in existence since 1914. I give special emphasis to the development of Hispanic Christian leadership amongst the Emerging Hispanic Generations since the early 1920s. Next, I will analyze the ethnic makeup of this Hispanic district, its philosophy of ministry, its constituency, and the challenges facing the nearly sixteen-year-old district in a post-*Christendom* and post-modern era.

Part D, Approaches to Leadership Development, presents a plan of action that may lead to Christian leadership development amongst the E.H.G. within Hispanic denominations. This section will identify five practical components leading to Hispanic leadership growth: (a) spiritual formation, (b) discipleship, (c) intergenerational outreach, (d) the formation of mentoring ministry, and (e) the creation of a Hispanic Center for Christian Leadership Development.

The fast growth of Hispanics within the United States, as well as the rapid church growth within Hispanic churches, underscores the need for new approaches, methods, and ministries. This requires that ministers and present leaders within our

Hispanic denominations need to be willing to engage in intentional Christian leadership development. More importantly, one task and goal needs to be in mind: that of enlisting more Hispanics within the E.H.G. as potential leaders for the twenty-first century throughout the Hispanic denominations' territory. Although this book makes reference to the Hispanics in the United States, it is important to understand that with the exception of the language barrier amongst the emerging generation, all of the Latin American Countries throughout the world will be facing the same challenges and needs. Therefore, this book could be useful not only in the United States, but also in every country facing generational challenges. To clarify, the usage of the term "leadership development" throughout this book is in reference to **Christian leadership development**.

Part A.

The Hispanic Context

One Saturday morning, while I was getting ready to go to my church's office to add the last touches to Sunday morning's message, I asked myself, "How about if I take care of my family first, and then take care of my Sunday morning message?" So I quickly came up with the idea of cooking an authentic Latin American breakfast dish. I remember mixing all the ingredients, from cherry tomatoes and black beans, to Latin sour crème and cheese: I felt like an authentic Latino chef. After serving the breakfast, we gathered around the table to say grace. My daughters' reaction was unexpected: "Dad", they said, "This food is delicious. What took you so long to cook a Latin breakfast for us?" It was at that time that I realized two things; the first was the fact that I passed the test as a cook, and the second, that this event should become a Saturday family tradition. Since that day, barring when I travel or am on vacation, I have been cooking the same Latin dish every Saturday.

Later that year during our Fourth of July celebration, I wanted to surprise my family with a Latin American barbecue. When I disclosed the menu to my daughters, they quickly replied, "But Dad, it is the Fourth of July; we are in the U.S.! We must have hamburgers and hotdogs." This incident made me realize that I have a wonderful family that is a mix of Hispanic and U.S. cultures. Krystal and Tiffany (my two daughters) were born in California, my wife was born in New York, her father was born in Cuba, and her mother in Puerto Rico. I was born in Guatemala, Central America, and came to the United States when I was nineteen years old. My daughters are a perfect example of the multifaceted background of their Hispanic generation, the Emerging Hispanic Generation (E.H.G.), which is the emphasis of this book. In order to obtain a better understanding of the emerging generation, it is essential to observe the rich and diverse Hispanic background surrounding this generation.

First of all, in the pursuit of familiarity and to become better acquainted with the language that will dominate this book, I would like to describe the E.H.G. as the subsequent generations (especially the third and fourth generations) that are emerging from those who immigrated to the United States. Most of the first generation group that came into the United States from Latin American countries is the "first generation" of Hispanics. Consequently, the term we use in regard to the Latino population within the United States is Hispanics instead of Latinos. Although we are conscious of the fact that both terms are interchangeable when referring to people of Latin American origin in the United States, I will use the term **Hispanics** through the entire book.

Secondly, as you read this book, I would like you to consider the process of drawing a set of blueprints. A set of blueprints consists of pages that an architect carefully draws in compliance with all city codes. The architect makes his drawings according to the design given by the company, institution, or the individual that has hired him. One of the architect's assignments is to make sure that his or her drawings reflect the vision and desires of the project's owner. When the drawings are complete, the architect presents

26

the set of blueprints to the project's owner. Each page of the blueprints serves to guide the workers toward the project's completion. Careful consideration should be given to the fact that the set of blueprints are never final, since they are subject to adjustments when necessary.

I would like to distinguish this present work as a set of blueprints that were drawn from previous Hispanic generations. I am not trying to redraw the current set of blueprints, for they have proven to be an effective tool towards leadership development for previous generations; rather, what I am proposing is a set of necessary adjustments or revisions to the old set in order to accommodate the E.H.G.'s need for leadership development within the Hispanic denominations throughout the United States, and throughout all the Latin Countries.

Before diving into the essence of leadership development as it applies to the E.H.G., it is beneficial to understand their background and socioeconomic characteristics, and the particular challenges that we face in the church environment. Let's begin by looking at the historical background.

Chapter 1

Background

The preliminary questions regarding the origin of the emerging generation are: Who are the Hispanics? Where do they come from? How did they arrive in the United States? What is the story behind their phenomenal growth in the United States? What are their socioeconomic challenges? And finally; what are the challenges facing the Hispanic churches between the first and the emerging generation of Hispanics? This chapter seeks to answer these questions through an overview of the Hispanic context within the United States. This synopsis includes but is not limited to: (a) Hispanic demographics, (b) socioeconomic factors, and (c) the intergenerational challenges between the first generation and the emerging generation.

HISTORICAL BACKGROUND

Where do Hispanics come from? Hispanic, as previously stated, is a term that identifies a group of people of Latin-American or Spanish origin living in the United States. The Hispanic population originated from colonies that once belonged to Spain, however, after the Mexican Independence, during the seventeenth century, such territories became part of the country of Mexico. It is important to point out that in the United States, a great part of the southwestern states such as Texas, New Mexico, Arizona, and California were not part of the United States of America during the seventeenth century, but rather part of Mexico.

The Hispanic population has lived in the southwest region of the United States since the early 1600s. Daniel Sanchez, in his book *Hispanic Realities*, says the following regarding the first group of Spanish Americans and its developments:

> Hispanics have been in the Southwest since the early 1600s. In 1528, explorations of what is now the Southwestern United States (New Mexico, Texas, and California) began. In 1598, Juan de Oñate (who married Hernán Cortez' niece) established the first colony in what is now New Mexico. Subsequently villas (provincial towns) were established in Santa Fe, Santa Cruz (Española valley), and San Felipe de Neri, which is now Albuquerque. In California, the famous mission along the California coast (the mission of San Diego), was founded in 1769 and Monterrey in 1770. By 1821, four principal areas of settlement had developed. The first and most heavily populated was New Mexico, consisting of towns, ranches, and farms. Next in size was California, consisting of missions, military fortress communities, towns, and ranches. Third was the northeastern settlement of Texas with its center in San Antonio. The smallest was the Arizona colony which was established in Tucson. Descendants of the colonial Spanish Americans

still live in California, Colorado, Arizona, New Mexico, and Texas.[1]

This quick historical overview helps us to understand that Hispanics have been an established population in the Southwest vicinity of the United States for the past four hundred years. Not all of the Hispanics within the United States have come from other countries. In fact, a group of already established people in the southern portion of the United States became U.S. citizens right after the United States obtained California and New Mexico from the Mexican Republic on February 2, 1848. The price paid for these states was fifteen million dollars. This treaty was "The Treaty of Guadalupe Hidalgo." During that time, "There were about 80,000 Mexicans living in the areas of California, New Mexico, Arizona, and Texas during the period of 1845 -1850, and far fewer in Nevada, in southern and western Colorado, and in Utah."[2]

During the past century, the United States experienced the beginning of what would eventually become a massive influx of immigrants. During the last decade, statistics show that four out of every ten immigrants who made the United States their home were Hispanic. Sanchez reinforces this point with the following statistics:

> Currently, four of every ten immigrants into America each year are Hispanics. The projection indicates that if this trend continues, in ten years half of all immigrants to North America will be Hispanic... the immigration rate of Hispanics in comparison to other cultural groups is phenomenal, in the year 2000 the black immigration rate was 10 percent, the American Indian, Eskimo, and Aleut was less than 1 percent, the Asian and Pacific

Islander was 28 percent, the Non-Hispanic White was 21 percent, and the Hispanic immigration rate was 42 percent.[3]

This group of immigrants would eventually be called Hispanics. Politics, civil wars, guerrillas, hunger, natural disasters, and socioeconomic factors have contributed to the migration of millions of people into the United States. Their place of origin is traced to Latin American countries within South America, Central America, North America (Mexico), the Caribbean Islands, and from European countries such as Spain.

NATIONAL DEMOGRAPHIC PORTRAIT OF THE HISPANICS

Population

As previously stated in the introduction, the Hispanic population in the United States is growing by the millions. According to the 2010 U.S. Census Bureau, the Hispanic population grew from about 35.3 million in 2000 to 50.5 million in 2010. As seen below in Figure 1, the Hispanic population has increased by more than 15 million people (43%) over the past 10 years.[4] In 2014 the Hispanic population grew to 55.4 million, and by the year 2060 will reach 119 million.[5]

The 2010 U.S. Census places the Hispanic population as the nation's largest and fastest growing minority group in the United States. It is remarkable to note that out of the 308.7 million people residing in the United States in 2010, the Hispanic population was the minority group responsible for over half (50.5 million, or 16 percent) of the United States' population increase,[6] and in 2014, the Hispanic population grew

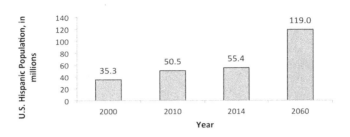

Figure 1. Hispanic population in the United States.

to 55.4 million. As seen below in Figure 2, the Hispanic population was the largest minority group living in the United States in 2014, comprising 18 percent of the total population, followed by African Americans in the second place with 12 percent, and Asians in the third place with 6 percent.[7]

The future for Hispanics in the United States looks promising. If the current demographic trend continues its course, by the year 2060, the Hispanic population in the United States will reach 119 million people. If this projection proves to be correct, the Hispanic community will not only continue to be the largest minority group, but more remarkably, will comprise upwards of 24 percent of the U.S. population.[8]

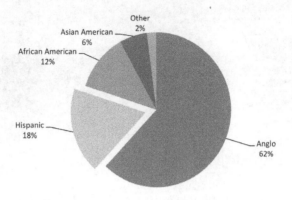

Figure 2. Population percentages of minorities.

Regardless of the challenges or the legal status facing the Hispanics, their future looks promising.

Hispanic Population by Region

Regarding the Hispanic population in the western part of the United States, the U. S. Census Bureau reports that "more than three-quarters of the Hispanic population have lived in the West or South" and that "in 2010, 41 percent of Hispanics lived in the West...Hispanics accounted for 29 percent of the population in the West."[9] Figure 3 shows the distribution of the Hispanic population by regions, showing the West containing the largest concentration of Hispanics in the United States. Regarding counties with a higher population, "The Census Bureau's annual population estimates detail the nation's demographics in a variety of categories, including race and ethnicity, geography, and age. For example, the county with the highest Hispanic population by far is Los Angeles County in California (4.9 million), followed by Harris County in Texas (1.9 million) and Miami-Dade County in Florida (1.8 million)."[10]

These statistics give us a clear picture of the Hispanic population within the United States, including the West, but more so the vast populations that our Hispanic churches and denominations need to reach.

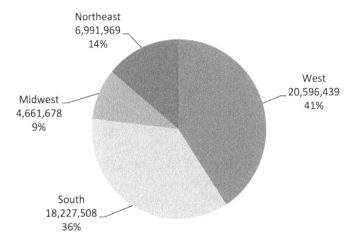

Figure 3. Hispanic population by region.

Hispanic Population by Type and Place of Origin

The Hispanic population living in the United States is well represented by different types and places of origin. Out of the 50,477,594 people accounted for in the 2010 Census, the country of Mexico has contributed to the majority of Hispanics in the United States with 63 percent, followed by Puerto Rico with 9.2 percent, Central American with 7.9 percent, South America with 5.5 percent, and Cuba with 3.5 percent.[11]

Hispanic Population by Gender and Age

The current generation of the Hispanic population living in the United States is generally quite young. The 2010 U.S. Census reports that 34.9 percent of the Hispanic population is less than eighteen years of age, in comparison to 65.1 percent that are over the age of eighteen. Only 5.8 percent are over the age of sixty-five, and 94.2 percent are less than sixty-five years of age. With regard to gender, over 25 million are males and close to 24 million are females.[12] The median white age is 42.1 in comparison with the Hispanic median age which is 27.2.[13] The median age of Hispanics, according to the new Census Bureau, is 29 years, up from 27 in 2010. In 2014 there were more Hispanics native born than those who were immigrants. "The majority of Hispanics in the United States are native born. Of the 55 million people in 2014 who identified themselves as of Hispanic or Latino origin, 35 percent (19.4 million) were immigrants."[14]

It is noteworthy to point out that nearly half of all children within the United States are from the minorities. In the 2010 census, 23.1 percent of all children living in the United States were Hispanic, compared to 14 percent for African Americans, 4.3 percent for Asians, and 3.8 belonged to the category of two or more races.[15] This remarkable statistic serves as a reminder that the size of the emerging generation of Hispanics is increasing.

SOCIOECONOMIC CHARACTERISTICS

Fertility Rates

One of the reasons for the greatest increase in Hispanic population in the United States is the fact that Hispanics traditionally had the highest fertility rate in the nation (fertility rate is the births per 1,000 women aged 15-44). The Hispanic fertility rate peaked at about 108 in 1990, whereas the non-Hispanic fertility rate that year was 67. By 2013, the non-Hispanic rate dropped to 60. The Hispanic rate has also dropped, to 73 in 2013, but is still significantly higher than the non-Hispanic rate.[16] This information is helpful, and it serves as a point of reference for those who may think that the only reason why the Hispanic population is growing is due to the immigration rate.

In 2013, the teenage fertility rate for Hispanics between the ages of 15-19 was 71, close to that of blacks that year (67), but far higher than that of whites (41).[17] The Hispanic birth rate among unmarried women in 2013 was 53, which was lower than that of blacks (71), but higher than the national average of 41.[18] The high birth rate among teens and unmarried women is an indication of the challenges facing the Hispanics in the United States.

Household Members and Income

One of the primary issues affecting every single social level of Hispanics in the United States is their high concentration of poverty. The Hispanic poverty level in the United States, while lower than in the past, is still of concern.

About 32 percent of Hispanics under age 18 live below the poverty level. This is in contrast to whites of the same age, whose poverty level is only about 13 percent. For the group between 18 to 64 years, 19 percent of Hispanics are living below the poverty line, in contrast to 10 percent of whites. Lastly, those within the category of 64 years and over had a 19 percent below the poverty level in contrast to 7 for whites.[19]

Hispanic households in the U.S., while decreasing in size, are still relatively large (26 percent of Hispanic households have more than five members as opposed to ten percent of white households), and along with their lower income level ($42,000 median income level, as opposed to whites at $59,200), this contributes to their relatively high poverty level.[20]

Education

Amongst Hispanics age 25 and older, 34 percent have not completed or obtained a high school diploma, compared to 8 percent of non-Hispanic whites; 27 percent have completed high school, compared to 28 percent of whites; 24 percent have earned some college or associate's degree, as compared with 30 percent of whites. With regard to a bachelor's degree, 14 percent of Hispanics, in comparison with 34 percent of whites, have received their bachelor's degree.[21]

The high school dropout statistics are better than in the past, but still not in favor of foreign-born Hispanics. The 2014 high school dropout rate amongst Hispanics between the ages of 16-19 was 6 percent, compared with about 5 percent for blacks, and 3 percent for whites. Of note is that the dropout rate for foreign-born Hispanics is 11 percent.[22] One might ask, "What are the reasons that foreign-born Hispanics have such a high rate of dropouts?" It would be difficult to single out only one reason when there are many factors to consider. The first issue that comes to mind is language.

Most first generation Hispanic families only speak their native language, which makes it difficult for them to help their children with school. Oftentimes, due to the language barrier, they are misinformed as to how to lead their children through the educational process that leads to higher education. In addition to this situation, the Hispanic students for the most part have to undergo a bilingual learning system, beginning with a program called ESL (English as a Second Language). Those students that get frustrated or don't manage to properly learn the English language are more than likely to become part of the dropout statistics.

Another issue that amounts to the high dropout rates amongst foreign-born Hispanics is the high level of poverty. A large percentage lives under conditions that do not allow them to have the right resources for a quality education. From improper nutrition to inadequate classroom settings, they find themselves in an educational atmosphere that lessens their chances to make it to higher education.

Sadly, the situation doesn't get any easier for many Hispanic students who are actively pursuing higher education. Due to the high cost of attending college, they often find themselves having to depend on scholarships, government grants, or loans in order to complete their degrees. Mark Hugo Lopez wrote an article, published by Pew Foundation in 2009, that is titled, "Latinos and Education: Explaining the Attainment Gap," where he brings up the reality as to why some Hispanics don't finish their college education:

> Nearly nine-in-ten (89%) Latino young adults say that a college education is important for success in life, yet only about half that number (48%) says that they themselves plan to get a college degree, according to a new national survey of Latinos by the Pew Hispanic Center, a project of the Pew Research Center. The biggest reason for the gap between the high value Latinos place on education and their more modest aspirations to finish college appears to come from financial pressure to support a family, the survey finds.[23]

Lopez's article describes the plight of many Hispanics, but thankfully, times are changing, and now Hispanic high school graduates are almost on par with whites in terms of attending some type of college. However, they are still less likely to attend four year colleges and selective colleges.[24]

Another important reason for the high rate of Hispanic dropouts is the combination of sex, drugs, gangs, and legal status. As mentioned previously, the pregnancy rate amongst Hispanics is high. When younger teens get pregnant at an early age, it makes it difficult to continue their education. These problems create a domino effect; subsequently, more Hispanic children would eventually end up getting involved with drugs, and especially gangs (approximately 44 percent of gang members in the United States are Hispanic, which is lower than in the past, but still higher than that of other ethnic groups).[25] Unfortunately, this leads to young people having low-paying jobs, thus, repeating the poverty cycle over and over again.

Language

The Spanish language dominates Hispanic homes. However, the emerging generation is either bilingual or prefers to speak English. The 2009 U.S. census report illustrates the discrepancy between first generation and emerging generation Hispanics, in terms of language preference. Within the U.S. Hispanic population between the ages of five through seventeen, 8.4 million speak Spanish and 7.8 million speak English. Among those age 16 through 64, 25.9 million speak Spanish and 17.8 million speak English. Among those age 64 and above, 2.6 million speak Spanish and 1.4 million speak English. When it comes to the English language spoken at home amongst Hispanics, between the ages of five through seventeen, 7,847,708 people speak English fluently.[26]

As you can see from these statistics, Hispanics over the age of 64, those for the most part who belong to the first generation, are the least likely to speak English.

SUMMARY

The demographic statistics clearly show that the Hispanics are making headway in the United States. The 55.4 million people who have made this country their home serves as a reminder that the task ahead of us is of mammoth proportions. This report helps us to understand that the offspring of the first generation of Hispanics, "The Emerging Generation," is growing rapidly; therefore, the Hispanic's leadership ought to make the necessary adjustments in order to accommodate and better serve this new generation.

STUDY QUESTIONS

1. Explain the meaning of the term "Hispanic."
2. What was the Hispanic population in the United States in 2014, and what is it expected to be by the year 2060?
3. According to the 2010 U.S. Census reports, what percent of the Hispanic population is less than eighteen years of age?
4. What is the percent of Hispanics under 18 years of age who live below the poverty level?
5. When it comes to the English language spoken at home amongst Hispanics, how many people speak English fluently?

DISCUSSION QUESTION FOR GROUP STUDY

What are some of the reasons why the emerging generation of Hispanics has experienced rapid growth in the United States?

CHAPTER PROJECT

Assign a group to do a demographic study of Hispanics in their community or state.

Chapter 2

Challenges

I can still remember it as if it was yesterday: it was one of the hardest challenges that I faced while pastoring a church in California. Our church's members were comprised of both English-speaking and Spanish-speaking people. The Hispanic Spanish-speaking congregation was younger than the English one. As the years went by, the English-speaking congregation became smaller than the Spanish-speaking one. After doing a careful survey of our congregation, some of the board members supported the idea of uniting the two groups into one and having only one service in Spanish.

This decision was perhaps the easy way out; however, my first concern was that at least half of the congregation consisted of children and youth belonging to the second and third generation of Hispanics. My heart was pounding, for included in that group of the younger generation were my own two daughters. It was in that particular moment that I began to realize that a Spanish-only service had the potential of discouraging not only the youth but also parents with small children. My proposal was simple and to the point, I said, "We cannot afford to conduct services in Spanish only at the peril of losing the younger generation whose primary language is English; furthermore, I will never support a worship service that could put my own children and yours in a predicament, where they may leave the church and move to the one next door that offers worship services in English."

We reached a compromise: we voted to have one bilingual service instead. Some members became upset and left the church; however, up until this day, I don't regret the decision. The children grew up, and at the present time, they belong to the youth group. In the same way, those who once belonged to the youth ministry became leaders in the church. Some of them are now part of the next generation of the Church's Corporate Board. The first generation of Hispanic leaders needs to understand the challenges as well as the differences between their generation and that of the emerging generation.

The quick overview of the demographics from the previous chapter gives us a foundation to better understand the challenges that lie ahead for the emerging generation. In general, the Hispanic Christian community is blessed with congregations that are aware of the crucial and pivotal need of leadership development for the E.H.G. Some churches have already begun the process of evaluating their congregations with respect to the multigenerational context. However, there are many churches that have yet to understand the Hispanic makeup of their respective churches.

To better understand this new generation and in order to achieve full effectiveness in the leadership development task, one must understand the differences between the First and the Emerging Generation of Hispanics. In what follows I would like to offer some light with regards to leadership development challenges facing the Hispanic churches in the United States.

I have chosen to use the church as an example, since most of leadership development training starts there. We can trace these challenges to the vast immigration of Latinos into the United States, the compound Hispanic context, and the birth of the emerging generation of Hispanics who are worshiping God within our Hispanic churches. It would be helpful to understand that the focus of this book is on leadership development for the E.H.G., taking into consideration that most of our churches have a Hispanic multigenerational group in their congregations, and the Emerging Generation is part of this group.

MULTIPLE GENERATIONS

I would like to make a distinction between the Hispanic and the Anglo generations. The first Hispanic generation is comprised of the first Latinos that immigrated to the United States. The 1.5 generation is the Latinos not born in the United States but brought to the country at a younger age. The second generation is the Hispanic born in the United States, and the third generation is the emerging generation. The subdivision of Hispanic generations is different from the Anglo ones, and so is the spectrum of ministry among each of them. For example, Sam Farina, an evangelist and certified coach, wrote an article called "Coaching Next-Generation Leaders." In this article he makes the following observation about the next generation of leaders and their task among four Anglo generations:

> The next-generation leaders will often work with four generations as ministry partners and the people they are reaching with the gospel: The silent (traditionalist) Generation, born before 1946; Baby Boomers, born between 1946 and 1964; Gen Xers, born between 1965 and 1980; and Millennials (sometimes called Gen Y or Generation Next), born after 1981. These four generations do not always communicate well with each other.[1]

Although some of the Hispanic generations could be part of the Gen Xers and Millennials, the Hispanic churches' membership makeup is comprised of at least two Hispanic generations that gather in the same building but with different characteristics. The first generation of Hispanics, as previously stated, includes the attendees who have migrated from the Latin American Countries into the United States. Their children are the Emerging Generation, especially the third generation. The second generation is the 1.5. This generation belongs to the group of Hispanics who were not born in the United States, yet immigrated into this country at a young age. For the most part, they have embraced the American lifestyle without forgetting their Latin roots.

Each generation has their own distinctive inclinations, likings, and challenges. The ability to work with all of them inside one building, while at the same time addressing a desire for them to join a leadership development program, requires a clear comprehension of their idiosyncratic context, as well as a careful study of their challenges.

WORSHIP

Effective leadership development should always include the study and practice of true worship. One may think that these issues, alongside with the ones that will follow, have no relevance with respect to leadership development. However, my experience visiting Hispanic churches as an itinerant evangelist as well as a pastor and executive presbyter in my denomination, leads me to underscore the importance of effective multigenerational worship as part of leadership development.

First generation worship style is totally different than the emerging generation one. Forcing the emerging generation to adopt the same worship style as the first can create frustration, and discourage Hispanic church attendance. To exemplify this

this point, allow me to illustrate some common scenarios, keep in mind that the old (first) generation of Hispanics prefers a traditional form of worship while the emerging generation desires a more contemporary one. The first generation is attracted to sacred music while the emerging generation is drawn by modern, rock, hip pop, and new age music.

Scenarios

Sometimes, the first generation is forced to listen to the music of the emerging one. This is often challenging because many members of the older generation find the new generation music to be stressful and even irreverent. Yet, the emerging generation is required to embrace and participate in the sacred or traditional music style. The first generation has no problem with extended worship services, but this is frustrating for the emerging generation who, for the most part, prefers a shorter version of it.

Technology used in the worship service might also be an issue. The first generation considers the physical copy of a Bible as sacred; therefore they carry it to church all the time along with their hymn book. In contrast, the emerging generation often relies on, and is satisfied with, their Bible app; furthermore, instead of carrying hymn books, they expect the lyrics to be displayed on the screen through a projector. The first generation does not need a sophisticated sound system or the latest technology in order to worship as compared with the emerging generation, who are used to high-tech equipment at schools or colleges.

Lastly, the first generation anticipates longer sermons that will culminate with an altar call, compared with the emerging generation who expect a more condensed and well-illustrated message that may or may not culminate with an altar call. Although these distinctive approaches to worship may not appear to play an important role in the quest for leadership development amongst

E.H.G., one needs to pay attention to this particular situation. There exists a possibility that as soon as they go off to college, they may not come back to a Hispanic first generation church. By making the necessary adjustments to accommodate their idiosyncrasies, we can pave the way for a much greater constellation of E.H.G. candidates for leadership development.

LEADERSHIP DEVELOPMENT STYLES

Most of the first generation of Hispanics comes from a Roman Catholic background, while others adhere to an Evangelical one.[2] Regardless of their theological or religious background, sometimes the emerging generation must embrace their ancestors' church and theology. They find themselves at war between American culture and the expectations of them as participants in the Hispanic Church. Some of them also find it hard to accommodate their parents' philosophies, theology, or ideas. Manuel Ortiz in his book, *The Hispanic Challenge*, gives more light to this dilemma when he says, "They are not integrating the faith of their parents. They do not have their own religion and their own expression of faith... they seem to be more ambitious than their parents and are attuned to the vibrations of the city."[3]

Even though this may be the case for a good portion of the emerging generation, I find the pendulum changing; there is a new desire amongst this generation to seek after their ancestor's religion. When the parents get involved and when the church also gets involved in the Christian upbringing of this generation, one can expect a good harvest of future Hispanic leaders within the emerging generation.

Ministers coming from Latin American countries often find themselves in conflict with the emerging generation in regard to leadership development. This conflict emanates from the different leadership approaches and training between these two generations.

For instance, sometimes the leadership style amongst the first generation is more of a non-relational style in contrast with the more relational style of leadership expected within the United States. Moreover, the first generation of ministers tend to be more legalistic, pragmatic, and resistant to modification, in contrast to the emerging generation that cries out for more understanding, flexibility, fellowship, and communication.

The emerging generation is more inclined to embrace a style of leadership that is more interactive. They would like to see the first generation leaders create a balance between the spiritual and the relational. To put it in a different way, they expect the first generation not to be too legalistic, serious, or pragmatic, and instead, open, humble, and social.

LANGUAGE BARRIERS

This issue is by far one of the most damaging between these generations. Language barriers can hinder the effectiveness of leadership development. In the previous section of this chapter, I observed that the primary language of the emerging generation is English. I have seen pastors and leaders repeatedly forcing the emerging generation to adhere to the Spanish language. Children and youth are pushed into a Spanish worship service that eventually would become irrelevant to them. The notion that the emerging generation can understand a little bit of Spanish opens a Pandora's Box of troubles.

Those leaders seeking a successful leadership development ought to understand that language can make a huge difference between failure or success when it comes to leadership development. The emerging generation responds more positively to the training in their native language, English. One need not to grasp the idea that their level of comprehension is limited, if not void, when forced to engage in training limited to a Spanish-only format. Undoubtedly, the first generation feels more comfortable when worshiping, training, or mentoring takes place in Spanish; however, compromising into at least a bilingual format will ensure more effectiveness. This is one of the reasons why churches and leaders conscious of this challenge before them have opted to transition Spanish format for the first generation and an English one for the emerging generation. Whatever the preference may be, one detail remains clear: the **Spanish-only format** would greatly hinder leadership development amongst the emerging generation, especially in churches with Hispanic multigenerational congregants.

SOCIOECONOMIC CHALLENGES

Hispanic immigration is real; as previously stated, four of every ten immigrants coming into America each year are Hispanics. Unfortunately, we cannot ignore the percentage of those immigrants who belong to the undocumented. There are possibly twelve million undocumented people in the United States. Although this claim is hard to prove, one thing is certain, and that is the fact that millions of undocumented Latinos have and will continue to make United States their home. The Pew Hispanic Center states the following statistics regarding undocumented immigrants in the United States:

> Unauthorized immigrants made up 30 percent of the nation's foreign-born population, about 4 percent of the entire U.S. population, and 5.4 percent of U.S. workers. Approximately 44 percent of the nation's unauthorized immigrants have arrived since 2000. About three-quarters (76 percent) of the 11.9 million unauthorized immigrant population are of Hispanic origin.[4]

A good percentage of Hispanics in this category have embraced our churches as their place of worship. This phenomenal scenario opens the way to many socioeconomic issues that may affect leadership development. To say that our Hispanic churches don't have undocumented Hispanics is downright erroneous. Hispanic leaders, ministers and even pastors deal with the ramifications of having undocumented congregants on a daily basis. Poverty, poor health conditions, low income ratios, and an emerging generation with a high percentage of dropouts greatly affect the church and the effective leadership development. An unfortunate case in point is the deportation trauma that family members within our churches often experience.

The implications of this situation can cripple the family, especially when the father or the mother is deported back to their home country, leaving children behind. How can you effectively train a young member of the emerging generation when his mind, heart, and soul are with his parents, who can no longer provide for his daily means?

This situation serves as an invitation to Hispanic leaders to engage in a dialogue that could result in strategies that can aid the undocumented community who, for the most part, love the Lord, the United States, and truly want to engage into leadership development.

IDENTITY

One last example of the many challenges facing the Hispanics attending our churches is that of identity. Most of the first generation of Hispanics has no problem tracing their origins to their native countries. However, the emerging generation is often troubled by their true cultural identity. They are Hispanics because of their ancestors as well as their last name; nevertheless, the reality is that the United States is their home, their community, and the

American culture is a tremendous influence. They may or may not eat tortillas, but they will surely eat hamburgers and hotdogs! However, the fact remains: they often feel they are neither "full Latinos" nor "full Americans."

This reminds me of one of the films produced by Walt Disney called The Jungle Book. In this film, the protagonist is a wild boy named Mowgli, who a panther named Bagheera finds in a basket in the forest. Bagheera immediately brings him to a mother wolf in order to raise him alongside her cubs, to be trained and accustomed to the ways of the jungle. Later, as a young adult, Mowgli follows a beautiful girl who leads him inside the village. After finding the girl, he begins to behave in ways that are contradictory to both his upbringing by his mother wolf, and his human nature. When the young girl says to him "You are a human" he pauses and then replies, "I am not a man and not an animal." In the same way, the emerging generation often characterizes itself as half Latino and half American. I see the product of two cultures, two countries, two sets of customs, and two different groups. Helping them to find their identity in the Lord, with an appreciation of their bicultural richness, would ensure healthy leaders amongst the emerging generation.

SUMMARY

The Hispanic context is heterogeneous, due in part to the richness of its people. In this section A, I have described the demographics surrounding the Hispanics. I especially emphasized the rapid growth amongst Hispanics during the last decade. This growth includes the E.H.G. Alongside these statistical findings, I have pointed out the socioeconomic factors affecting Hispanic Americans, particularly those of the emerging generation. Finally, I have also analyzed the challenges that confront the Hispanic churches. Some of these challenges are: worship styles, leadership styles, language barriers, and socioeconomic challenges. The pre-existing findings and challenges affecting the Hispanics serve as vital tools for those seeking an effective leadership development. In the next section I will take a journey throughout the Bible in search of leadership development examples amongst great Bible characters that can serve as a foundation for effectively training the E.H.G.

STUDY QUESTIONS

1. In what country are the second and third generations of Hispanics born?
2. What is the form of worship desired by the emerging generation?
3. What is the leadership style that the first generation sometimes adopts?
4. What is the primary language of the emerging generation?
5. How does the emerging generation feel about their true identity?

DISCUSSION QUESTION FOR GROUP STUDY

What are some of the leadership development challenges facing the Hispanic churches in the United States regarding the emerging generation?

CHAPTER PROJECT

I have presented at least four major challenges confronting the Hispanic churches in relation to the new generation. Identify two or more of these challenges and come up with possible solutions.

Part B.

The Bible And Emerging Leadership

The Lord has given me the privilege of ministering in different parts of the world. Every country has its own unique beauty and history. One of the countries that I will never get tired of visiting is Israel. Its vast and rich culture, and its connection to our Christian heritage, draws me in at all times. There is one place in particular in Israel that holds special value for the authenticity of the Old Testament, and that place is the Qumran Caves. It is the place where a young shepherd discovered the Dead Sea Scrolls in 1946. The manuscripts found in these caves date back to at least the third century BC. Some of the manuscripts contain fragments of the Old Testament books of the Bible. The Dead Sea Scrolls serve as a testimony to the fact that the Bible is not only the Word of God but also a historical book written thousands of years ago.

Today, it is important to find translated manuscripts of the Old and New Testaments that can testify to the origins of biblical leadership development. In the Old and New Testaments, we can find what I would call the **Old Prints for Emerging Leadership Development.** Let us open these translated manuscripts in order to understand the biblical background for emerging leadership development.

Chapter 3

Old Testament

O ur God is a God that loves, embraces, and practices leadership development. Since the beginning of time, God has desired to establish among His people a nation that will honor Him, follow His commandments, and carry out His message through subsequent generations. One of the strategies used by God in this endeavor is the one of leadership development. The theme of leadership development throughout the Bible is not limited to the first generation of leaders, for in its narrative the Bible includes leadership training for the emerging generation. In the Old Testament one can observe leadership development in action through the stories of Moses and Joshua and also Elijah and Elisha. In this chapter I bring attention to the leadership development amongst the emerging generation within the Old Testament. Let us now take a bird's eye view of the biblical characters of the Bible, with the goal of directing others towards God's desires and purposes for His people.

We will start with a proper understanding of the term "leadership" from its biblical perspective in the Old and New Testaments, which I think is essential, because the more familiar both pastors and lay leaders are with its meaning, the more training they can draw from each of the Bible's leadership narratives.

According to the Exhaustive Concordance of the Bible, the Hebrew term used in the Old Testament for leadership is יָד *yad*. It has approximately 1,614 occurrences. Three of its main translations are: "hand, consecrate, and power." The word *yad* denotes amongst other things possession, power, and control. These meanings are linked with one of the main translation which is "hand"[1] The *Theological Wordbook of the Old Testament* explains that the term "hand" is used for a person performing many functions at his or her own will. "From a theological standpoint, the term hand is put to use in an idiomatic manner suggesting or conveying 'responsibility, care, and dominion over someone or something. One may be under the custody of this authority'"[2]

The other Hebrew word used with regard to leadership is נָגַד *nāgad* meaning, "tell, and make known." Its derivatives are:

נֶגֶד *neged*, which means "before," and נָגִיד *nāgid*, which means "ruler, leader, and captain."[3] The *Theological Wordbook of the Old Testament* states that the basic root for the word *nāgad* indicates, "to place a matter high, conspicuous before a person."[4] The synonymous, as well as the theological, meaning of this verb indicates God's calling to an individual to whom He gives information of interest to share with His people. This information bears God's purpose and divine message for His people.[5] Therefore, according to the Old Testament perspective, a leader is a person who is called, consecrated, and empowered by God to lead, to guide, and to tell. Moreover, he or she is a person who makes God's message known and is purposed for His people. The leader is given the responsibility to not only guide and lead, but also to care for God's people under his or her custody or authority.

With regard to the term "development", the *Concise Oxford Dictionary* defines the word as "the process of developing or being developed and a specified state of growth or advancement."[6]

This growth often comes at a progressive or gradual pace and its main aim is maturity. Effective Christian leadership development includes the understanding that a leader should always strive to use God's given capacities, gifts, and abilities. He utilizes his hands symbolically for the purpose of leading others towards achieving God's plans and desires.

I concur with Robert Clinton's definition of a Christian leader. In his book *Leadership Emergence Theory*, he gives the following definition of leadership emergence that includes capacity, responsibility, and leadership to achieve God's plans for His people. He states, "A Christian leader is a person with God-given capacity and God-given responsibility who is influencing a specific group of God's people toward God's purposes."[7] Biblical leadership was understood to be sacred and was not to be taken lightly. Those called to the role of leadership were often assigned younger apprentices with the goal of training them to become the future generation of leaders. Such is the case of some biblical characters like Moses and Joshua, Elijah and Elisha, Jesus and His disciples, and Paul with Timothy.

Christian leadership development has been in existence for thousands of years. The Old and New Testament are full of narratives that can best describe the development of leadership from a biblical perspective. The proper understanding of biblical accounts can serve as a valuable tool in leading us toward the implementation of an effective leadership development amongst the Emerging Hispanic Generation (E.H.G.). One needs to understand that leadership development is a process, not an event. Such processes are found through vivid examples carried out by the biblical characters in the Word.

MOSES

Moses is one of the most prominent leaders of the Old Testament. His first assignment carried a message of deliverance. One of the best-known Bible verses of all time is the depiction of Moses's oracle regarding God's plan to deliver the Hebrews from Pharaoh's oppression, saying, "Thus says the Lord, the God of Israel, 'Let My people go, that they may celebrate a feast to Me in the wilderness'" (Exodus 5:1 NASB). Another assignment was to lead God's people out of bondage and into the Promised Land (Exodus 3:17), and to receive God's law and deliver it to the people of Israel (Exodus 19, 20). God gave Moses the authority and the power to use the staff in his hands not just to lead, but also to perform wonders (Exodus 4:1-5; 14:21; 17:6). God gave Moses the honor and holy task of building His tabernacle in the wilderness (Exodus 25:1-9). Last but not least, Moses received a direct command from God: to train Joshua as his successor and as the future leader who would take God's people into the Promised Land (Deuteronomy 31:14, 23).

Moses's Leadership Development

The Bible identifies Moses as a leader. His leadership is embraced throughout the emerging generations. Numbers 33:1 speaks about Moses's leadership, saying, "These are the journeys of the sons of Israel by which they came out from the land of Egypt by their armies, under the leadership of Moses and Aaron." The paramount task and leadership position given to Moses didn't take place overnight. The leadership development of this leader was nothing short of a lifetime process. It started in Egypt and concluded in Mount Nebo, which accounts for at least eighty years of constant leadership training. All of the years experienced by Moses, from the moment he had his first encounter with God at

Mount Horeb to the miracle of the burning bush (Exodus 3) and to the time of his death (Deuteronomy 34), were years in which he received never-ending lessons and experiences on leadership development.

Moses was a first generation leader whose leadership development training was a collection of commands given by God, plus personal experiences throughout his journey in the wilderness. At the top of Mount Sinai, he had unique and personal encountered with God (Exodus 19). He also endured disappointing moments, an example would be when his own people died due to their own stubbornness (Numbers 21:4-8). Moses's leadership is the epitome of the Hebrew word *yad* (hand, consecrate, power, authority, leadership). I can observe within the biblical narratives that throughout Moses's leadership journey he used his hands to lead God's people and perform wonders. His journey also revealed that leaders are not perfect, yet God still loves and uses them.

Moreover, Moses was neither a perfect person nor a perfect leader. Before his first encounter with God at Mount Horeb, he was a runaway criminal (Exodus 2:11-14). He broke the first tablets of the law that God gave and wrote (Exodus 32:16-19). He disobeyed God's instructions by striking the rock twice (Numbers 20:9-12), and in spite of his repeated pleas, to enter into the Promised Land, God declined Moses's request to enter the Promised Land and commanded him not to insist anymore (Deuteronomy 32:48-52). Even though Moses was not a perfect man or leader, he was a man full of love for God's people. Moses's desire was to see Israel follow God's commands and acquire His favor, as they journeyed toward the Promised Land. Paul J. Kissling, in his work, *Reliable Characters in the Primary History*, says the following concerning Moses desires for God's people:

> While much of Moses's speech in Deuteronomy relates to the task of warning Israel against future

disloyalty to Yahweh, this passage [Deuteronomy 33] makes it clear that in doing so, Moses was genuinely concerned for the welfare of the nation and genuinely wanted Israel to heed his warnings and receive the ensuing blessing of Yahweh.[8]

We can safely concur that Moses was a man full of love for God and for His people. God loved Moses, too; He communicated with him "face to face" and was counted as one of the unique and powerful prophets in Israel's history (Deuteronomy 34:10).

MOSES AND JOSHUA:
AN EXAMPLE OF EMERGING GENERATION
LEADERSHIP DEVELOPMENT

Moses's contribution towards his emerging generation can be traced back to the moment he took Joshua under his wing. Nowhere in the narratives of the Bible have I seen Moses as a selfish leader wanting to restrict others from learning. When God commanded Moses to develop leaders that could help with his endless task of judging the people, he never refused, instead, he followed His command (Deuteronomy 1:9-15). Once again, Moses selfless character is shown when he obeyed God's instruction of choosing Joshua as his successor. (Deuteronomy 31:14, 23).

Moses's Leadership Training with Joshua was Successful

One of the last verses recorded in the book of Deuteronomy gives an account of the successful leadership training between Moises and Joshua. Near the end of Moses's life on earth, he laid hands (*yad*) on Joshua and released him as Israel's new emerging leader, "Now Joshua the son of Nun was filled with the spirit of wisdom, for Moses had laid his hands on him; and the sons of

Israel listened to him and did as the Lord had commanded Moses" (Deuteronomy 34:9).

Moses's leadership development strategies are shown throughout his personal training with Joshua during Israel's journey towards the Promised Land. This training included theory as well as personal experiences that would eventually form Joshua's character. Eventually, Joshua took Moses's position as Israel's new leader and in doing so, the cycle of leadership development for the emerging generation had taken its course.

Moses Selected Joshua as His Helper

In the book of Numbers, I observed that the people able to serve in the army were over six hundred thousand men journeying towards the Promised Land (Numbers 1:46). Perhaps out of this big number, Moses selected one young man to be his servant, thus beginning Joshua's training for leadership as a member of the emerging generation. Selection is of great significance when engaging in leadership development, "So Moses arose with Joshua his servant, and Moses went up to the mountain of God" (Exodus 24:13). Joshua was able to serve Moses, and was ultimately rewarded by experiencing God's presence in a more intimate way.

Moses Showed Joshua the Importance of Seeking God

Moses's life as a leader displayed much fasting, prayer, and seeking God's direction. His servant Joshua learned at a young age about the importance of prayer as well as seeking God for guidance: "Thus the Lord used to speak to Moses face to face, just as a man speaks to his friend. When Moses returned to the camp, his servant Joshua, the son of Nun, a young man, would not depart from the tent" (Exodus 33:11). Every time Moses entered the tent to inquire of God, the people of Israel would also enter into their own tents to worship. However, when Moses would exit the tent, I read that Joshua (his young aide) would not leave the tent. Moses's communion with God influenced Joshua; he learned the importance of seeking God and worshipping Him at all times.

Moses gained Joshua's trust. his life impacted Joshua in such a way that he never departed from serving his master throughout his youth. His faithfulness to God in spite of his shortcomings, disappointments, or even great accomplishments showed Joshua how to endure hardships and how to remain faithful to the task: "Then Joshua the son of Nun, the attendant of Moses from his youth…" (Numbers 11:28). Joshua saw in Moses the modeling of endurance, faithfulness, servanthood, and leading by example. He learned from Moses how to be a true servant of the Lord.

Moses Released Authority and Leadership

Moses's love for Israel led him to make a request to the Lord for a leader to take his place. God instructed him to take Joshua and lay hands (*yad*) on him to begin the process of releasing his authority into Joshua (Numbers 27:15-23). What I find remarkable about the passage is the fact that Moses as the leader of Israel released part of his authority unto Joshua while he was still alive.

He was not only obedient to God's command, but more so content with His decision. Nowadays, it is sad to see some leaders who prefer to wait until they are nearing death before they can start the process of releasing authority unto the younger generation. Moses's success in leadership development is a testament to the fact that the young boy (Joshua), who was once his servant, would now take his place, leading Israel into the Promised Land (Numbers 14). Eventually God gave Joshua leadership, authority, and encouragement to go forth and possess the Promised Land (Joshua 1:9). At the end, through Joshua's leadership, Israel conquered and possessed the Promised Land. May the Hispanic generation of leaders follow after Moses's footsteps by training and releasing the next generation of leaders.

ELIJAH

Moses was the leader chosen by God to take Israel into the Promised Land, and Elijah was a prophet sent by Yahweh to remind Israel that idolatry was not the right path to find God's favor. As a leader, Elijah (who's name in Hebrew means "my God is Yahweh") was empowered by the Lord to show Ahab, Jezebel, and Baal's prophets that there was only one powerful and true God in Israel, and that His name was and forever will be Yahweh.

One glance at the Bible's narrative about Elijah would help us to conclude that, although he was far from perfect, God still used him in a powerful way. His leadership is remembered as one of great deeds and miracles. From his first arrival at King Ahab's palace to his unique departure to heaven, he was an instrument used by God to do signs and wonders. Matthew Henry's *Commentary on the Whole Bible* makes the right assertion that sometimes our character will match our assignment; such was the case of Elijah's before King Ahab and his wicked wife Jezebel. Henry states,

> *He was a man subject to like passions as we are* (James 5:17), which perhaps intimates, not only that he was liable to the common infirmities of human nature, but that, by his natural temper, he was a man of strong passions, more hot and eager than most men, and therefore the more fit to deal with the daring sinners of the age he lived in: so wonderfully does God suit men to the work he designs them for. Rough spirits are called to rough services. The reformation needed such a man as

Luther to break the ice. Observe, 1. The prophet's name: *Elijahu— "My God Jehovah is he"* (so it signifies), "is he who sends me and will own me and bear me out, is he to whom I would bring Israel back and who alone can effect that great work."[9]

I agree with Henry's commentary on how God deals with our character by molding us for ministry. One thing I know about Elijah is that in spite of his humanity, he showed faithfulness and obedience to God until the end. Elijah's assignment allowed him to perform miracles of great proportion: he prayed for multiplication of oil and flower while visiting the widow from Zarephath (1Kings 17:13-16); he prayed for the resurrection of a child and God answered him (1Kings 17:17-24); he predicted a drought in Israel (1Kings 17:1); he confronted the prophets of Baal and challenged them to pray to their god's for fire, but when he prayed for fire, God answered him by sending fire from heaven (1Kings 18:36-38); he prayed for rain and God sent the rain upon his people (1Kings 18:41).

ELIJAH AND ELISHA:
AN EXAMPLE OF EMERGING GENERATION
LEADERSHIP DEVELOPMENT

Prior to Elijah's ascension to heaven, God gave him an assignment: to call and train Elisha as his successor (1Kings19:16). The meaning of the name Elisha in Hebrew is "my God is Salvation." The Bible doesn't record the exact length of time of the leadership training given to Elisha; however, it is clear that by the time of Elijah's ascension to heaven, Elisha was ready to take on his mantle (the baton), continuing the legacy of leadership as a prophet amongst the people of Israel. This task would take him toward continuing the development of prophets for future generations.

In the same way that Moses was instructed by God to choose Joshua as his successor, Elijah was also instructed by God to choose and anoint Elisha as his successor (1 Kings 19:16-19). From the moment that Elijah threw his mantle over Elisha, the process of leadership development for Elisha had begun. What are some of the valuable lessons that I can draw from this narrative with respect to leadership development?

Obedience to God at All Times

Elijah learned how to listen and be obedient to God's command. There is no record in this narrative that would lead us to believe that Elijah argued about God's candidate; rather, he was obedient to His choice for his replacement: "So he departed from there and found Elisha, the son of Shaphat, while he was plowing with twelve pairs of oxen before him, and he with the twelve... And Elijah passed over to him and threw his mantle on him" (1 Kings 19:19). This verse shows us that yielding to God's will and accepting His leadership choices are signs of total obedience towards Him.

A Lesson in Humility and Love for God's Leaders

By surveying the precious leadership journey taken by Elijah, We are able to identify him not only as a man of bad temper, but more so as a passionate prophet that loved God, Elisha, and the future generation of prophets. At the end of his leadership journey, knowing that his time of departure was near, he took a path that would lead him into his ascension to heaven. In this journey, He passed through Gilgal, Bethel, Jericho, and Jordan (2Kings 2:1-8).

Why is it that Elijah asked his servant and leader in training to stay in Gilgal? Some have suggested that since Elijah knew that the Lord was about to take him to heaven, he wanted to accomplish two things: first, to pay his last visit and farewell to the schools of the prophets, including the ones that he established (Bethel); and second, to ask his leader in progress, Elisha, to stay behind. His request was not one of being rude or cruel, but rather one that perhaps will show humility and a desire to be alone in order to prepare for his departure. Elisha's decision to continue walking with his master was never denied; furthermore, Elijah would never deprive his servant from spending his last moments on earth alongside with his mentor. Jameison and others, in *A Commentary, Critical and Explanatory, on the Old and New Testaments* says the following regarding this unique occurrence:

This Gilgal (Jiljil) was near Ebal and Gerizim; a school of the prophets was established there. At Beth-el there was also a school of the prophets, which Elijah had founded, notwithstanding that place was the headquarters of the calf-worship; and at Jericho there was another (2Ki 2:4). In travelling to these places, which he had done through the impulse of the Spirit (2Ki 2:2, 4–6), Elijah wished to pay a farewell visit to these several institutions, which lay on his way to the place of ascension and, at the same time, from a feeling of humility and modesty, to be in solitude, where there would be no eye-witnesses of his glorification. All his efforts, however, to prevail on his attendant to remain behind, were fruitless. Elisha knew that the time was at hand, and at every place the sons of the prophets spoke to him of the approaching removal of his master. Their last stage was at the Jordan. They were followed at a distance by fifty scholars of the prophets, from Jericho, who were desirous, in honor of the great occasion, to witness the miraculous translation of the prophet. [10]

The experiences of love and humility lived by Elisha while serving Elijah was valuable and foundational for his leadership development.

Passing the Baton to the Next Generation of Leaders

Elijah was an extraordinary leader. His ascension to heaven serves as an example that although he was not perfect, he walked with God in faithfulness, humbleness, and obedience. Just before he was taken to heaven and after crossing the Jordan, he asked his disciple what he could do for him, "When they had crossed over, Elijah said to Elisha, 'Ask what I shall do for you before I am taken from you.' And Elisha said, 'Please let a double portion of your spirit be upon me.'" (2 Kings 2:9). This verse demonstrates that the time for Elisha's promotion had arrived. He had passed the test, concluded the training, and now he was ready to receive the baton of leadership from his mentor. In spite of the fact that Elisha's request was a hard one (v.10), Elijah gives him hope, and was willing to release his mantle, or leadership inheritance, to Elisha. One cannot help but observe the contrast between verses 2 and 11. The former is a plea aimed towards Elisha to stay at Gilgal; the latter is an affirmation that if Elisha stays with Elijah and sees his departure, his request would be granted.

When graduation time took place, Elisha was left not only with a mantle in his hands but also with the spirit of Elijah resting upon his life (v.12-15). Not only did Elisha experience God's anointing when he crossed the Jordan by striking the waters, but more so: the school of prophets bore witness to his miracles and received him as a leader. There are many ways to interpret the wonders that followed in the life of Elisha, but history would record numerous miracles performed by the apprentice that surpassed the master. This story of Elijah and Elisha is a vivid example of what leadership development is all about.

SUMMARY

We have taken a quick overview of two leaders who passed the mantle of leadership onto the next generation. Moses and Elijah, like us, were imperfect human beings. However, their love for God, and strong relationships with Him, allowed them to flourish in their capacities as models for leadership development. The older generation of Hispanic leaders will do well by learning from the Old Testament characters that leadership development is in the heart of God, and that the task of choosing future leaders is at hand. Let us now proceed to the New Testament in search of biblical characters whose roles were influential in the area of leadership development for the emerging generation.

STUDY QUESTIONS

1. What does the synonymous, as well as the theological, meaning of the Hebrew verb for leadership (*nāgad*) indicate?
2. What is Robert Clinton's definition of a Christian leader?
3. What did Moses as the leader of Israel release unto Joshua while he was still alive?
4. In 2 Kings 2:9 we see that the time for Elisha's promotion had arrived. He had passed the test; concluded the training. What is it that Elisha was ready to receive from his mentor?

DISCUSSION QUESTION FOR GROUP STUDY

What can the older generation of Hispanic leaders learn from Old Testament characters in relation to mentoring the emerging generation?

Chapter 4

New Testament

I n the New Testament, Paul speaks of leadership development when writing to the Ephesians. He emphasizes the roles and the objectives of the leaders chosen by the Lord to serve in the church for the equipping of the saints and for the building of the body of Christ. The following verse describes what leadership development is all about: "And He gave some as apostles, and some as prophets and some as evangelists, and some as pastors and teachers, for the equipping of the saints for the work of service, to the building up of the body of Christ" (Ephesians 4:11-12).

The New Testament narrates the stories of leadership development through the relationship between Jesus and His disciples, Paul and Timothy. In this chapter I will bring attention to the leadership development of the emerging generation within the New Testament Bible characters previously mentioned. I will also underscore the role of the Holy Spirit within leadership development. There are more New Testament characters who can serve as examples for leadership development; however, I have chosen the above characters because of their distinctive task of empowering the emerging generation of leaders within their context.

JESUS AND HIS LEADERSHIP LEGACY

The Old Testament's narrative ends with writings belonging to Minor Prophets and their unending appeals to the people of Israel to follow after God's commandments. The last writing of the Old Testament warns Israel about the great day of the Lord, yet in the same book, the prophet Malachi issues an oracle of hope for those who fear the name of the Lord and those who are willing to live a life of righteousness (Malachi 4:1-2).

The next narrative belongs to the New Testament. Its first chapters narrate Jesus's genealogy, placing him as the "Messiah" or the "Anointed one" (Matthew 1:1). Jesus Christ would become the first leader of the New Testament that would choose twelve people to become His disciples, and in doing so, He marked the beginning of a new era of leadership development. What is remarkable about this particular New Testament narrative is the fact that in the past, the Lord instructed leaders such as Moses and Joshua, and prophets such as Elijah and Elisha, to urge Israel to follow the Lord's commandments. This time around, it would be God Himself who will come to lead, instruct, and die on behalf of mankind. The Greek word used in the *Dictionary of Biblical Languages with Semantic Domains* for leader or to lead is ὁδηγός *hodēgos*, which means leader or guide. The Greek word *hodēgéō* means "to lead," "to show the way," "to instruct."[1] All of the characteristics found in the word *hodēgéō* were accomplished in the life of Jesus Christ while on earth.

Another term directly related to leadership development is "**empowerment**." The Greek words related to empowerment are *energeō* and *energēma* which mean "function, cause to function, grant the ability to do work, deed" (1 Corinthians 12:6, 10, 11 ESV). The other word related to empowerment is *exousia*, which means "power to do something, implying authority." Jesus was given power and authority, and in the same way He empowered

His disciples to go, make disciples, and to baptize them. He empowered them for ministry. (Matthew 28:18-19)[2]

Jesus Christ is by far the best example of what leadership development should be. The proof of His success as a leader and as a mentor rests in the fact that His disciples became the leaders of the Primitive Church, and we Christians are the fruit of His leadership. The numbers of leaders emerging from His leadership while He was on earth are countless. Let us view some of His leadership development strategies found in the New Testament.

LEADERSHIP DEVELOPMENT STRATEGIES USED BY JESUS WITH HIS DISCIPLES

Jesus Christ's leadership success was due in part to the way He mastered His discipleship training. One glance at the four Gospels will testify to the effectiveness of His approaches toward mentoring and developing leaders. Jesus Christ was aware of the short time available to Him while on earth. Every occasion became a lesson and a new strategy to be observed. His training was intentional; He was fully aware of the fact that His disciples would become the next generation of leadership in the years to come. In spite of the countless strategies worth analyzing, I will only discuss a few in this chapter, and mention a few more in the last chapters of this book.

Choose Ordinary People Who Would Eventually Become Extraordinary Leaders

The twelve candidates for leadership chosen by Jesus were nothing more than ordinary people. Among the group, we find fishermen such as Peter, Andrew, and John (Matthew 4:18-20); a tax collector, Matthew (Matthew 9:9); and a traitor named Judas, to name a few (Mark 3:19). Jesus chose His disciples, notwithstanding their humble backgrounds, without any animosity, prejudice, or discrimination. Jesus understood that some of them had previously followed John the Baptist, but was aware of the fact that each and every one of them had the potential of becoming the next generation of leaders who would eventually transform the world with His gospel.

Jesus Christ was a risk-taker. No experienced leader in search of his dream team would ever begin a group by choosing the ordinary ones first; however, Jesus was a firm believer in moving from the ordinary to the extraordinary. A. B. Bruce, in his work, *The Training of the Twelve*, confirms the fact that this cluster of twelve were chosen not only to be trained by the Lord as future leaders, but most importantly, as leaders that would be trained to the extraordinary office of apostleship. Bruce states,

> The twelve entered on the last and highest stage of discipleship when they were chosen by their Master from the mass of His followers, and formed into a select band, to be trained for the great work of the apostleship.[3]

This strategy used by Jesus serves as a reminder that anyone called to the office of leadership has the potential to do great things for God's kingdom.

Effective Leadership Training Embraces Friendship

Those of us that believe in leadership training are often confronted with the great peril of not leading by example. In my personal journey of leadership I have come to the conclusion that leadership development will always require friendship and fellowship with those who are leading. John (the beloved), an apostle of Jesus Christ, was one of His disciples who testified to the friendship and fellowship that he experienced with his Master Jesus Christ. In the gospel bearing his own name, he testified of the personal and intimate relationship Jesus had with His disciples: "And the Word, *Jesus* [name added for emphasis], became flesh, and dwelt among us, and we saw His glory, glory as of the only begotten from the Father, full of grace and truth" (John 1:14). Jesus's disciples not only received His personal training, but also experienced His company, love, and compassion. Jesus ate with them, walked with them, slept among them, and finally suffered death for them.

An effective leader is one who is willing to gain the confidence of his followers by becoming their friend. Jesse Miranda's book, *Liderazgo y Amistad* (Leadership and Friendship), proposes a leader as a "principal-friend who lives with integrity in society, practices intimacy with his followers as Jesus did"[4] (author's translation from Spanish).

This strategy is a vivid illustration reminding us that effective leadership training embraces not just theory, or lectures, but a personal relationship between the one leading and the one following.

Prayer

One of the unique characteristics of Jesus's training was the great value that He placed on prayer. Quite often in the Gospel, we find Jesus secluding Himself to spend time alone with His father. Nevertheless, although He was the son of God, as a human, He understood the importance of connecting and reaching intimacy with His father. For example, Jesus learned the importance of prayer and He taught His disciples how to pray (Matthew 6:9-13); He also advised His disciples on the importance of fasting (Matthew 6:16-18). Finally, Jesus always longed to be in solitude with His father (Matthew 14:23); even the cross was not able to stop the communication between Jesus and His father. Four out of the seven words uttered from the cross were directly aimed to His father.

In Acts 2:42-47, we find His disciples praying, seeking the Lord, and seeking communion and intimacy with Him at all times. Jesus would always take time out of His busy schedule to be alone with His father, the disciples understood this. After Jesus's departure to heaven, they also practiced prayer, fasting, and intimacy with God. Indeed, prayer is a foundational component for effective leadership development. Jan Johnson, in her book, *Spiritual Disciplines Companion*, reminds us of the importance of spending quality time with God. She states:

> Some may wonder why Jesus would need a pattern of private getaways while living on earth as a human being. Hadn't he already spent eternity in fellowship with the Father? This puzzled even the disciples, who are portrayed in the Gospels as having to find Jesus when he had gone away to pray…But his urgency and frequency hint at something better-he sought solitude simply because he longed to be alone with God.[5]

Servanthood

The following Bible passage describes the role of every leader when he or she is training the next generation of leaders, and that role is the one of servanthood:

> But it is not this way among you, but whoever wishes to become great among you shall be your servant; and whoever wishes to be first among you shall be slave of all. For even the Son of Man did

75

not come to be served, but to serve, and to give His
life as a ransom for many (Mark 10:43-45).

Servitude is a valuable leadership strategy. Jesus Christ gave
to His disciples many vivid lessons on the importance of serving
instead of being served. From His humble conception to His crucifixion, He showed His disciples by His example that in leadership,
it is better to serve than to be served. One of the classic examples
of servitude from the Lord is found in John 13:4-11 when Jesus
surprised His disciples by washing their feet. When Peter opposed
such a humiliating act, Jesus took the opportunity to show him and
the rest of his fellow disciples that the life of a leader should be
one of humility and service at all times. Only by learning how to
serve first, will a leader be able to understand that serving others is
a privilege and an act of obedience to the Lord's command. Robert
Greenleaf, speaking on the priority of serving others in *Servant
Leadership* said,

> The natural servant, the person who is servant first,
> is more likely to persevere and refine a particular
> hypothesis on what serves another's highest pri-
> ority needs than is the person who is leader first and
> who later serves out of promptings of conscience or
> in conformity with normative expectations.[6]

This strategy used by the Lord permeated the disciples' future
approach to servanthood. After Jesus's death, His disciples followed after their Master; they sacrificed their own lives for the
sake of Christ.

Evangelism

Jesus understood the importance of evangelism. In Luke 10:1-20, Jesus instructed His disciples on effective evangelism. Let us look at some of His instruction that can be applied to effective leadership development training. He sent them in pairs and to every city, with the understanding that the harvest was ready, yet the ones willing to gather it were few; He warned them about the dangers of evangelism. They would be like lambs around wolves. He also warned them about the importance of traveling light, and to trust in God for their needs. He told them to bring peace to the houses they enter, and to announce that God's kingdom has come to them. This is leadership development that focuses on, not only theory but also practice.

The seventy disciples came back with good news, and Jesus celebrated their success by reminding them that although the demons were subdued in His name, their names are noted in heaven, and that was a reason for them to rejoice. Evangelism is important, as so is proper training. To send people to evangelize without the appropriate instruction is not wise. Evangelism is one of the areas responsible for Hispanic growth; therefore, it is vital to study and to apply Jesus's strategies with the Emerging Hispanic Generation (E.H.G.). I will discuss the importance of evangelism in Chapter 10.

THE APOSTLE PAUL

The Apostle Paul was a leader called by the Lord to minister to the gentiles (Acts 9:15). During the lifetime of his leadership, he was able to develop various laypeople into leaders. One of the leaders responsible for Paul's own leadership development was Barnabas. According to the Scriptures, Barnabas went to Antioch to look for Paul, and for at least one year Barnabas trained and prepared Paul for ministry:

"And he left for Tarsus [Barnabas] to look for Saul; and when he had found him, he brought him to Antioch. And for an entire year they met with the church and taught considerable numbers; and the disciples were first called Christians in Antioch" (Acts 11:25-26).

In short, Paul became a noteworthy leader whose contributions to Christianity are valued immensely. Paul's leadership legacy includes: (1) writing, Paul was one of the authors of the New Testament; (2) missions, Paul established new churches throughout the Roman Empire; and (3) mentoring, Paul mentored Christians that would eventually become pastors, missionaries, historians, and leaders in the churches he established.

PAUL AND TIMOTHY:
AN EXAMPLE OF EMERGING GENERATION
LEADERSHIP DEVELOPMENT

Paul trained many leaders for ministry, and among them, Timothy is a notable example of the importance of training the next generation of leaders. During his first missionary journey, Paul met Timothy under extreme circumstances. Nevertheless, Timothy became Paul's companion from that moment on, and Paul poured out his leadership experiences onto Timothy. As a result, Paul's investment in Timothy's life eventually paid off. While there are many leadership strategies that we can draw from Paul's ministry, let us examine some of the strategies used by Paul in the course of Timothy's training.

Endurance

Paul's encounter with Timothy was God's providence. It came after a beating that nearly killed Paul. This instance was not the only one in which Timothy was able to observe Paul's endurance, especially among the worst of circumstances. People who, instead of becoming partners in ministry, opted to destroy Paul's labor in ministry, constantly attacked him. Nevertheless, Paul remained faithful to God's work and to those who the Lord placed under his mentorship's wings. In his first letter to Timothy, Paul admonishes him to observe and practice endurance until the end:

> For this reason I *endure* [italics added] all things for the sake of those who are chosen, so that they also may obtain the salvation which is in Christ Jesus and with it eternal glory. It is a trustworthy statement: For if we died with Him, we will also live with Him; If we endure, we will also reign with Him; If we deny Him, He also will deny us; If we are faithless, He remains faithful, for He cannot deny Himself (2 Timothy 2:10-13).

One of the lessons that we need to give while training the next generation is the one of endurance. As Christian leaders, it is good to remember that the world we live in will always require dependency on the Lord in order to stay on course, even throughout hostile situations.

Genuine Love

Paul's love for all of his leaders in training was genuine, especially his love for Timothy. From his first encounter with Timothy in Lystra (Acts 14:8-23; 1 Timothy 1:2) until his last instructions (2

Timothy), Paul expressed love towards him. Some scholars believe that part of the second letter that was written to Timothy included Paul's last will (2 Timothy 4:6-8). He remembered Timothy at all times. In fact, he called him "my beloved son" and yearned to see him. Moreover, this recollection of Timothy's tears was an uplifting remembrance that brought him joy in the midst of his persecutions:

> To Timothy, my beloved son: Grace, mercy and peace from God the Father and Christ Jesus our Lord. I thank God, whom I serve with a clear conscience the way my forefathers did, as I constantly remember you in my prayers night and day, longing to see you, even as I recall your tears, so that I may be filled with Joy (2 Timothy 1:2-4).

In his first letter to Timothy, Paul made it clear that the goal of his instructions included love. He says, "But the goal of our instruction is love from a pure heart and a good conscience and a sincere faith" (1 Timothy 1:5).

You may ask, "How does love relate to leadership development?" Love is an essential component, Pastors, leaders, and lay-people can benefit greatly from each other as they learn to add a loving relationship to their training. Our next generation needs to feel love from their mentors. They need to see that we care for them by having them in our prayers, in our minds, and in our hearts. The next time someone suggests that we should not get too close or emotional with those who we are training, we ought to tell them: "I want to imitate Jesus's and Paul's love for their mentees."

Active Participation

Paul's leadership approach included hands-on training. In his first letter to Timothy, he gave assignments to his protégé by appointing Timothy to instruct and to teach (1Timothy 1:3; 4:11). He entrusted Timothy with the care of the churches that he had established. The confidence he had in Timothy was evident. Through their relationship we learn that the office of the teacher is important in leadership. We often put a lot of emphasis on the office of a pastor, but we forget that teaching is also a ministry. In fact, teaching is the Holy Spirit's gift for the "equipping of the saints for the work of service, to the building up of the body of Christ" (Ephesians 4:11-12). Paul was neither afraid nor jealous of releasing Timothy for ministry. In the same way, the pastors and leaders in our churches ought to feel the need to release laypeople into ministry. Most importantly, the next generation of leaders is in need of our trust. As we train them, they expect to gain our confidence and to be trusted with ministry opportunities.

Develop a Leadership Manual

The overview of the two letters written to Timothy can serve as the foundation for a leadership development manual. Paul used this method while training his mentees. His training approach was specific and instructional; he left no room for misunderstandings or confusion. Verbal training is good, but the need for written instructions or manuals for leaders is also important. God left us with an instruction manual, and in the same way it is important to leave a manual for the next generation of leaders. As we look at Paul's manual for leadership, which we find in the two letters written to Timothy, we see instructions on a number of subjects. Here are some subjects that are covered in the first letter:

Faith and conscience (1:18)
Prayers (2:1-8)
Women's behavior (2:9-15)
The office of overseers and deacons (chapter 3)
Discipline (4:6-10)
How to be an example to others (4:11)
The importance of reading the Scripture (4:13)
Relating to elders (5:17-23)

In the second letter addressed to Timothy, Paul gives his beloved disciple some last minute instructions. His last charge to Timothy was to preach the word at all times, and to reprove, rebuke, and exhort (2 Timothy 4:2). Lastly, he instructed Timothy to endure hardship while doing the work of an evangelist (4:5). The valuable lessons found in Paul's letters to Timothy serves as a reminder that leadership training is for life. It requires endurance, love, practice, and a manual that contains guidelines.

THE ROLE OF THE HOLY SPIRIT IN THE BIBLICAL EMERGING GENERATION

The Holy Spirit has played an important role in leadership development. From the time of the creation of mankind (Genesis 1:2) until the end of times (Revelation 22:17) the Holy Spirit has been present.

The Holy Spirit in the Old Testament

In the Old Testament we see the Holy Spirit descending upon particular leaders and enabling them to do ministry or particular tasks. Oftentimes in the Old Testament the Holy Spirit is known as "The Spirit of the Lord" (Judges 14:6), and "The Spirit of God" (Genesis 1:2). We can find examples where the Spirit came upon

David (1 Samuel 16:12-13) and Saul (1 Samuel 10:10, when the Spirit specifically enabled Saul to prophesy), and others. In the lives of Moses, Elijah, and Elisha, we see the manifestation of signs and wonders taking place due to the Spirit's empowerment (Exodus 14:1-31; 1 Kings 18:36-38; 2 Kings 4:32-37), and in Joshua, I see God's Spirit upon his life when Moses is instructed to lay his hands on him (Numbers 27:18).

The Holy Spirit in the New Testament

...but you will receive power when the Holy Spirit has come upon you; and you shall be My witnesses both in Jerusalem, and in all Judea and Samaria, and even to the remotest part of the earth (Acts 1:8).

The first chapters of the book of Acts, narrates what took place after the Lord's ascension into heaven, and it was the ingathering of 120 people at the upper room seeking the power of the Holy Spirit (Acts 1:12-14). In this group, eleven out of the Lord's twelve disciples were present. They gathered in the upper room as an act of obedience to the Lord's command to be there and wait for the power of the Holy Spirit to fall upon their lives.

The future leaders of the Primitive Church received an **empowerment** for ministry and leadership. They were commanded by the Lord to go preach the gospel and to make disciples. The following are some examples of the Holy Spirit's role in leadership development, as recorded by Luke in his book of Acts:

Empowerment: 120 people were filled with the Holy Spirit and began to speak in other tongues (Acts 2:1-4).

Preaching: Peter's messages, after been filled with the Holy Ghost, resulted in salvation for at least eight thousand people (2:41; 3:25); the Primitive Church was established and the next generation of leaders began their training, which included seven men of good reputation, full of God's Spirit and wisdom (2:42-47; 6:1-6).

Signs and wonders: The Holy Spirit enabled the new generation of leaders to perform signs and wonders (2:43); the proclamation of Christ surpassed Jerusalem's boundaries, and made its way to the Gentiles and the rest of the world (8:4-16; 10:34-48); the conversion of the apostle Paul took place in such an unprecedented way that, after being filled with the Holy Spirit, Paul would become the apostle called by God to minister to the Gentiles (9:15-17). Paul belonged to the next generation of leaders; and at the same time, he trained and developed those of the emerging generation (Timothy, Luke, Titus) for leadership and to continue the proclamation of the Gospel of Jesus Christ.

The Holy Spirit has always played a vital role in leadership development. He was present and active in the Old Testament, as well as the New Testament, by empowering leaders for service and allowing them to use the gifts available to them in order to carry out their God-given task. May our new generation of leaders allow the Holy Spirit to empower them for service in the same way He did in the Old and New Testament.

SUMMARY

We have taken a bird's eye view of the Old and New Testament in search of leadership development. I have also presented the strategies used by Moses, Elijah, Jesus, and Paul. These strategies were effective and successful, resulting in a great harvest of leaders from generation to generation until today. We conclude this chapter and section B, with the following observation: Hispanic leadership development can be more effective if we are willing to realize the importance of its development throughout the biblical narratives. We should embrace the practice and usage of the principles found in the Bible as valuable tools towards proper leadership development within our Hispanic denominations. In the next section, I will present a case study of the Assemblies of God denomination, including the history behind leadership development amongst Hispanics since the 1900s, and a brief review of the formation of a Hispanic Latin American district.

STUDY QUESTIONS

1. What is the Greek root word for "leader," found in the Dictionary of Biblical Languages, and the original Greek definition of this word?
2. What is the meaning of the word "empowerment" according to the Greek words *"energeō," "energēma,"* and *"exousia"*?
3. Jesus was aware of the fact that His disciples had the potential of becoming what?
4. Name one of the areas responsible for Hispanic growth in the United States.
5. What are the two qualities that Jesse Miranda (in his book Leadership and Friendship) proposes for a good leader?

6. Name at least two of the strategies used by Paul in the course of Timothy's training.

DISCUSSION QUESTION FOR GROUP STUDY

What is the role of the Holy Spirit in leadership development?

Part C.

Case Study: The Assemblies Of God

O ne of the best ways to understand leadership development is to analyze how it has been applied within a denomination over the course of many years; to observe the successes and also the inevitable challenges, and to learn from them. You are now familiar with both the biblical basis of leadership development and the Hispanic context of the Christian faith in the U.S. In the following chapters, we will take a look at how a large and growing Hispanic denomination implemented these biblical teachings. This case study includes a brief history of the Pentecostal development of the Assemblies of God. I give special emphasis to the leaders that paved the way for the prosperous Latin American movement, whose overall membership is nearly 292,000. In the last chapter of this section, I will analyze a Hispanic District by the name of the Northern Pacific Latin American District (NPLAD). I will review its demographics, its philosophy of ministry, and finally the challenges surrounding this seventeen-year-old district.

Chapter 5

Pentecostal Development In The United States

If there is one family that qualifies as a beautiful blend of various Hispanic cultures, it is my own. I am blessed with a family that represents at least four countries: Guatemala, Puerto Rico, Cuba, and Spain; we love to go on vacation and to visit different countries whenever finances will allow us. Every year we gather together at the dinner table to decide the place we will visit during our vacation. Everybody has an opinion, every vote counts, and at the end majority wins.

A few years ago, one of my daughters suggested we go and visit a country of her ancestors. The country that won the vote was the one in which I was born (Guatemala). Tiffany said, "Dad, you always say that you were born almost at the altar inside the church's parsonage. I want to visit the exact place and room where you were born." That was a challenge, since the parsonage where I was born had already been remodeled a few times. After arriving at the international airport in Guatemala, we drove to the place where I was born. We managed to go inside the house, and visit the room where I was born. Tiffany was satisfied and overwhelmed to see the place.

It is important to know where we come from. Our history and our background serve as points of reference to our heritage. In the same way, it is important to know our Christian background and the humble beginnings and heritage of our denominations. Let us take a tour of the rich heritage of a denomination called the Assemblies of God.

The Assemblies of God is one of the largest Pentecostal denominations in the world, with a constituency in the United States of over 3 million, and over 67 million worldwide.[1] It was established in the United States in 1914. This denomination was not responsible for the beginning of the Pentecostal movement, but rather for the unification of Pentecostal leadership under one fellowship. The formation of Pentecostalism in the United States can be traced back many years prior to the formation of the Assemblies of God.

Some of the events that led to the development of the Pentecostal movement were the spiritual revivals during the First and Second Great Awakenings. These events paved the way for Pentecostal trailblazers to strive voraciously for new spiritual outpourings. The Brief History of the Assemblies describes their insatiable needs in the following way:

> Pentecostal pioneers were hungry for authentic Christianity, and they looked to previous spiritual outpourings such as the First Great Awakening (1730s-40s) and Second Great Awakening (1800s-30s), for inspiration and instruction. They identified themselves in the tradition of reformers and revivalists such as Martin Luther, John Wesley, and Dwight L. Moody.[2]

One of the leaders who was responsible for the beginnings of the Pentecostal movement in the United States was Charles F. Parham. He was a Methodist minister and had pastored a church in Kansas. His desire for God to use him in a greater dimension led him to open a new ministry in Topeka, Kansas, in the year 1898. The name of this ministry was The Bethel Healing Home. Afterward, Parham opened a Bible school and began to teach a small group of students on the subject of spiritual gifts. He believed that if these spiritual gifts were still accessible, God would give these gifts not only to him but to his students.[3]

Parham instructed his students to study the Bible with the goal of finding scriptural proof that can substantiate the reception of the baptism of the Holy Spirit. After their arduous search, Parham's students found that such evidence could be corroborated in the Book of Acts. From that moment on, they began to open their hearts to the baptism of the Holy Spirit.

In the beginning of the twentieth century the first manifestation of what Pentecostals call the baptism of the Holy Spirit, with the evidence of speaking in tongues, took place at a watch night service. During this service, a Bible student by the name of Agnes N. Ozman requested Parham to pray for the baptism of the Holy Spirit to fall on her. On the first day of the twentieth century, she began to speak in tongues. Peter Wagner, a leading authority in the field of evangelism, in his book, *Your Spiritual Gifts Can Help Your Church Grow* calls this event the beginning of the "Classical Pentecostal movement." He states:

> The roots of this new thing began in 1900, the most widely accepted date for what is now known as the classical Pentecostal movement. During a watch night service, beginning December 31, 1900, and ending on what is technically the first day of the twentieth century, Charles Parham of Topeka,

Kansas, laid his hands on Agnes Ozman, she began speaking in tongues, and the movement had begun.[4]

THE ORIGINS OF THE ASSEMBLIES OF GOD

One of the factors that lead a group of ministers to organize a gathering in 1914, was the need to have a movement whose main characteristic was the baptism of the Holy Spirit, with the evidence of speaking in tongues. Shortly after, all ministers and missionaries received an invitation to attend the General Council in Hot Springs, Arkansas. In spite of opposition by the conservative movements of that time, 300 leaders, ministers, and missionaries answered the call. Some of the leaders who attended represented different Pentecostal organizations, such as: the Christian and Missionary Alliance, Dowie's Zion, Chicago's various missions, Parham's Apostolic Faith, and the Alabama-based Church of God in Christ.[5]

The General Council took place from April 2-12, 1914. One of its most significant outcomes was the formation of a fellowship whose primary purpose was "to recognize Scriptural methods and order for worship, unity, fellowship, work and business for God and to disapprove of all unscriptural methods, doctrine and conduct." The delegates who attended this Council voted to incorporate this new organization under the name of "General Council of the Assemblies of God."[6]

The Assemblies of God believes in evangelism, discipleship, and missions. God has truly blessed this movement. The 2014 Assemblies of God U. S. Vital Statistic reports a total of 675 Sections, 12,849 churches, and a total membership of 1,812,126. Additionally, 13.3 percent of this membership consists of boys, 14.5 percent girls, 31.5 percent men, and 40.6 percent women. Their total major worship attendance is 1,927,575, the total adherents is 3,146,741. Out of this report is it important to highlight the fact that **22.5** percent (**706,570**) of the Assemblies of God's adherents is of a Hispanic origin. Their worldwide statistics shows 360,074 churches and 67,290,023 adherents.[7]

Their Hispanic Districts' vital statistics are as follows: **2,118 churches**, a total **membership of 292,972**, including 45,123, boys, 51,579 girls, 121,410 men, and 159,276 women. The number of adherents is 379,388 and the major worship attendance is 272,708.[8] This number could be greater, because about 20 percent of Hispanic churches do not send their vital statistics reports.

THE HISTORY OF LATIN AMERICAN ASSEMBLIES OF GOD

One of the saddest Old Testament narratives is in the book of Judges. **It is the story of an emerging generation that followed after Joshua died. They did not have a personal knowledge of God, and did not know what the Lord had done for Israel** (Judges 2:10). The consequences were catastrophic. The book of Judges tells us that they "did evil in the eyes of the Lord and served the Baals" (Jud. 2:11). They "prostituted themselves to other gods and worshiped them. They quickly turned from the ways of their ancestors, who had been obedient to the Lord's commands" (2:17), they had no leader, and would not listen to the judges assigned by God. As a result, "…everyone did what was right in his own eyes" (Judges 17:6).

Those who belong to today's emerging generation need to have a personal relationship with God. They need to hear and see what God has done through previous generations. They should know their background and their heritage. They ought to get acquainted with the former leaders in their denominations who left marks in the old blue print of leadership. Who were they? Where did they come from? How much did they sacrifice in order to give birth to a Hispanic denomination that has impacted the world with the gospel of Jesus Christ? Let us take a look at some of those heroes, and learn from their approaches to leadership development.

H. C. Ball

The history behind the Latin American Assemblies of God's formation is rich. Its background is traced to the 1910s, when a young man by the name of Henry C. Ball accepted God's calling to open a Hispanic mission in Ricardo, Texas. Ball's endeavor was rewarded with the birth of thousands of Hispanic churches that have made the Assemblies of God their home.

Ball was born in Brooklyn, Iowa, on February 18, 1896. Throughout his life he faced many obstacles such as illnesses (spinal meningitis, rheumatism, and lung troubles) and the loss of his father when he was only eight years old. Nonetheless, God had a plan for his life. In 1908, wanting the best for her son, Ball's mother, a Christian woman attending a Methodist church, and his grandfather, took a long journey in a wagon pulled by three burros (donkeys) that eventually culminated in a little town in Texas called Ricardo. After purchasing a piece of property, this community became the place where Ball would experience a life-changing transformation.[9]

Ball's Call to Ministry

While Ball was attending high school, one of his teachers, who was a Christian, led him to the Lord on November 6, 1910. Soon after his conversion he began attending Christian conferences in which he would hear a missionary from Venezuela speak and minister God's Word. The result of these meetings produced in him a genuine call to do missionary work among the Mexican community. Ball was not aware of the paramount ramifications of such a ministry. His outreach at a schoolhouse not only affirmed God's

94

calling to his life and ministry among the Hispanic community, but more so, it paved the way for the birth of the now nine Hispanics Districts within the Assemblies of God.[10]

Ball didn't have a preceding ministerial experience before having services at a schoolhouse, but his passion for a Hispanic ministry and the encouragement of a Methodist minister kept him determined to continue. In his first service only two people attended: Mrs. Juanita Bazán and Mr. Villareal. His order of services was humble, as Bruce Rosdahl, in his article "Whatever the Cost: The Formative Years of H. C. Ball, Pioneer of Hispanic Pentecostalism," states:

> Ball sang the one Spanish hymn, read the Lord's Prayer, sang the same hymn a second time and then had Mrs. Bazán [first name Juanita][11] read a few verses from Romans 12. After she read from the Bible, Mrs. Bazán and the gentlemen spoke for some thirty minutes. Ball could not understand the conversation, but he later discovered that Mrs. Bazán, though a devout Catholic, had attended some Protestant services and was explaining some of the beliefs to the man.[12]

Ball's work was blessed when Juanita's husband started coming to the services and gave his life to the Lord, thus becoming Ball's first convert. By the year 1912 at the age of sixteen, Ball received his license to preach from the Methodist denomination, and on November 7, 1914, he received the baptism of the Holy Spirit. Shortly after this, he joined the Assemblies of God movement. On January 10, 1915, at the age of seventeen, Ball was ordained as a minister of the Assemblies of God. Ball's arduous work and faithfulness to God is reflected in his seventy-four years of ministry in the Assemblies of God that will forever be remembered.[13]

95

Our beloved pioneer understood the need for Hispanic literature, biblical education, church planting, and leadership development. Through his endless devotion and efforts, he was able to leave a legacy.

Publishing

After publishing his first Hispanic tracks in 1915, he went on to establish the first Hispanic Evangelical Publishing House in 1924 named Casa Evangélica de Publicaciones (Gospel Publishing House). This publishing house was able to print tracks, Sunday school material, textbooks, and a magazine called La Luz Apostólica (The Apostolic Light); Hymnology. Ball was a person whose passion for Spanish music and hymns lead him to translate many English songs into the Spanish language. As a result, in 1916 he published a Spanish hymnal book called Himnos de Gloria (Hymns of Glory); which has made its way to every Latin American country. Moreover, his hymnal became one of the first Pentecostal hymn book in the United States.

New Missions

After his successful work among the Hispanic community in Ricardo, Ball went on to open many missions around the state of Texas that eventually became churches. One of his effective leadership strategies was to train Hispanic national workers and to install them on each of the new missions. The Assemblies of God appointed him as the superintendent of Hispanic works in 1918.

Latin American Bible Institute

With the rapid growth of emerging churches in the state of Texas, the need to open an institution that could train Hispanics into future ministry and leadership was evident. Once again, Ball met this need by establishing the first Hispanic Bible Institute. In 1926, with the help of his wife, Sunshine, and Alice Luce, two Hispanic Bible centers were opened. Eventually, this institution took on the name of Latin American Bible Institute (LABI). I will forever be grateful to this pioneer who has left us with this leadership training institution. LABI was my first training ground, and now I see myself committed to take part in the training of the E.H.G.[14]

Leadership

The young man who couldn't yet speak Spanish answered God's calling to his life among the Hispanic people. He was a pastor, publisher, Christian educator, hymnologist, church planter, and the superintendent of Hispanic work. Finally, in 1929, he organized the first Latin American District Council where he was elected the first Superintendent of the new Hispanic District. H. C. Ball's legacy can best be summarized with the words written by Bruce Rosdahl: "Ball is representative of those early entrepreneurial Pentecostals missionaries whose vision and courage superseded the obstacles they encountered."[15]

Demetrio Bazán

One of the leaders trained by Ball was Demetrio Bazán. He was the first Hispanic Superintendent among the Latin American Assemblies of God. He was born on December 22, 1900, in the state of Tamaulipas in Mexico.[16] Prior to Bazán's conversion, when he was a young teenager, he would occasionally visit Ball's church in Kingsville, Texas, not to worship but to cause disruption outside of the church. However, one rainy night while he tried to find shelter, he found himself inside Ball's church and listened to

Alice E. Luce speak, who was a missionary in India. The Lord convicted Bazán and he gave his heart to the Lord on June 1917. After proper leadership training and mentoring, Bazán became Ball's church assistant.[17]

After three years, Bazán's passion for the Lord and his continual faithfulness to his mentor was rewarded on May of 1920, when he was ordained as a minister of the Assemblies of God alongside with his wife Nellie, only months after their marriage.[18] Ball was used by God to establish the Latin American Assemblies of God, and his successor Bazán would take this Latin Council into a new level. In 1939, nineteen years after his ordination, Bazán became the first Hispanic superintendent of the Latin American District Council. Ball, his predecessor, served as the superintendent since its formation in 1929 until 1939.[19]

Bazán and his wife were visionaries and believed in empowering the next generation of leaders. As an evangelist and church planter, he would pitch a tent and then go from street to street, inviting people to the evangelistic services. Once a group of converts was formed, they would choose a young man with a passion and desire to be used by the Lord and would place him in charge of the new converts until a new pastor would arrive. By using this system, many churches were established in different parts of Texas. In 1932 his desire to see more churches planted and his unconditional dependence in the guidance of the Holy Spirit took him to Colorado. After pastoring a prosperous church of 400 people, he felt God's calling to resign the church and move to a place he never knew existed. His wife Nelly Bazán, recalled Demetrio Bazán's words:

> Una tarde del mes de Agosto de 1932, iba a visitar a
> la familia Robles por una calle solitaria. De repente
> sentí una impresión que yo denominaría como una
> visión. Me dijo: 'Irás a Denver.' Busque por todos

lados para ver si alguien me hablaba, pero no ví a
nadie.[20]

(One afternoon during the month of August 1932,
while on my way to visit the Robles family, down
a lonely street, suddenly I felt an impression that
I would call a vision. It said: "You will go to
Denver." I searched everywhere to see if someone
spoke to me, but I did not see anyone.)

Bazán's obedience to the voice of the Holy Spirit paved the
way to numerous Assemblies of God churches being founded in
Denver, Colorado.

Reorganization

During Bazán's tenure, the Latin American District was reor-
ganized from eleven conferences to four and the full-time conference superintendents were placed in its respective zones. This
strategy allowed greater evangelization and more effective administration. Another important reorganization attributed to Bazán
was the relocation of the two Bible schools. One school was relocated from Saspamco to Ysleta, Texas, and the other school from
East Los Angeles to La Puente, CA. The formation of the Spanish
Eastern District was due in part by the efforts and suggestion of
Bazán; his efforts would pay off in 1956 when the new district was
established. On January 1959, after many years of hard and endless
work, his secretary Jose Girón was elected as a new superintendent
of the Latin Assemblies District, after being trained and mentored
by Bazán. It was a position that he held until 1971.[21] Girón, who
at the time of Bazán's death had become the Superintendent of the
South Pacific Latin American District, summarized Bazán's leadership legacy best in his eulogy:

Hubo un hombre enviado por Dios, el cual se llamaba Juan (Juan 1:6). Los que conocemos la obra del Concilio Latinoamericano nos hemos familiarizado con el ministerio de Demetrio Bazán. Apreciamos la obra que hizo, y continuaremos diciendo que "hubo un hombre enviado de Dios, el cual se llamaba-en este caso- Demetrio Bazán."[22]

(There was a man sent from God, whose name was John [John 1:6]. Those who knew the work of the Latin American Council have been familiarized with the ministry of Demetrio Bazán. We appreciate the work that he did, and will continue saying that, "There came a man sent from God, whose name was-in this case-Demetrio Bazán.")

Bazán was a trailblazer, whose life and arduous work paved the way for hundreds of Hispanic leaders presently serving not only in our District, but all over the world.

José Girón

Girón was born in Del Norte, Colorado, in 1911. Before becoming a superintendent, he pastored various churches in Colorado, New Mexico, and California. In 1936, while working as a presbyter of the New Mexico conference, he had an experience that nearly cost him his life. After a glorious service in a church at a town called Gallina (chicken), Girón, along with a lay worker named Miguel Sanchez, was wounded by three gun shots. Though Girón was shot in the neck, he survived; unfortunately, his companion died from his wounds.[23] A group of people who disliked the Pentecostal movement plotted against Girón's life and ultimately killed an innocent bystander.

Girón was a man whose devotion to Christian education was evident. He obtained a degree in theology from Light House Bible College of Rockford. He was responsible for taking the Latin American Bible Institute to a higher level. I had the privilege of meeting him in person, and when I expressed my desire to be in the ministry, he encouraged me to continue my education at LABI. The Lord used Girón to see the Latin American District subdivided into four more districts at the 47th District Council, held in Albuquerque, New Mexico, in 1971. The names of the newly formed districts were: Gulf Latin American District, Midwest Latin American District, Central American District, and the Pacific Latin American District. Girón went on to write constitutions for each district and served as a superintendent for the Southern Pacific Latin American District (SPLAD).[24]

This brief history of the founding leaders of these movements serves as a reminder that leadership development has and will continue to harvest more leaders and membership in the years to come. The work is not easy, yet it is rewarding. The sacrifices made by these leaders have paved the way for a prosperous Hispanic denomination, as well as great leaders within the Hispanic Assemblies of God movement.

In the next chapter we will review the development of a Latin American District within the Hispanic Assemblies of God, called Northern Pacific Latin American District.

STUDY QUESTIONS

1. How many Assemblies of God adherents are of a Hispanic origin according to their 2014 report?
2. How old was H.C. Ball when he received his license to preach, and when did he join the Assemblies of God movement?

3. Who was the first Hispanic superintendent among the Latin American Assemblies of God?

DISCUSSION QUESTION FOR GROUP STUDY

In this chapter, we have followed the story of two key leaders behind the Latin American Assemblies of God. Can you identify the main leaders that paved the way for the formation of your denomination?

Chapter 6

Northern Pacific Latin American District Formation

Although the Hispanic Pentecostal movement is traced back to the twentieth century, the missionary work among Hispanic Protestant Churches in the Southwest has been in existence since the 1820s. Mainline protestant churches such as the Presbyterians, Methodists, and Baptists have played an important missionary role.[1] The earliest efforts made by Hispanic Protestants to establish themselves as a Missionary Society based in California dates back to 1897. Clifton Holland, in his work, *The Religious Dimension in Hispanic Los Angeles*, writes about the Hispanic Protestant origins in Southern California:

> One of the earliest known Protestant efforts to establish an organized ministry among the Spanish-speaking people in Southern California was the creation of the California Missionary Society. This interdenominational society was organized in 1897 through the vision and determination of Alden B.

Case of Pomona. Case became the society's first 'general missionary' and wrote a pamphlet in June 1897, entitled Foreign Work at Home for Our Spanish Neighbor, in which he and his supporters stated their case for developing evangelistic work among the Hispanic population.[2]

The first preacher who came out of the Apostolic Faith Mission in Los Angeles was Juan Navarro.[3] The founder of this church was William Seymour, who was a disciple of Charles Parham. Shortly after he was baptized in the Holy Spirit, Seymour went on to lead an unprecedented manifestation of the Holy Spirit called the "Azusa Street Revival." Many Hispanics who attended the Azusa Street Revival, which took place during the early 1900s, gave their hearts to the Lord and were also baptized. Bartleman, in his book *Azusa Street*, states that this event "ushered into being the worldwide twentieth-century Pentecostals renewal. From this single revival has issued a movement which by 1980 numbers over 50,000,000 classical Pentecostals in uncounted churches and missions in practically every nation of the world."[4]

Francisco Olazaval was another preacher who ministered through the U.S. South Region; he was a pastor in California during the early 1900s. He was baptized in the Holy Spirit in Oakland, California, and he played a vital role in the early stages of Hispanic Pentecostalism.[5]

DISTRICT FORMATION HISTORY

The Southern Pacific Latin American District (the first Assemblies of God Hispanic District in California) was formed in 1971 at the 47th District Council, which was held in Albuquerque, New Mexico. The first superintendent was Girón, and he inherited eighteen churches with an approximate membership of 1,080.

Their first offices were located in La Habra, California. Later on they relocated to La Puente, California, until today. During Girón's tenure as SPLAD's superintendent, the district continued its growth. Since then, SPLAD has given birth to two more districts. After Girón's retirement, one of his trainees and secretary by the name of Jesse Miranda became the new SPLAD superintendent.

Jesse Miranda

Jesse Miranda was born in Albuquerque, New Mexico. He grew up in a poor barrio among junk cars, marijuana, and gangs. His father was a sawmill worker from the Mexican state of Chihuahua, and his mother was of Spanish descent with a third grade education. At the age of twenty-one Miranda left New Mexico and embarked on a journey to California that would prove to be successful. He has received various degrees including a Doctor of Ministry from Fuller Theological Seminary. His knowledge and expertise regarding Hispanic culture is shared in the two books he has written, *The Christian Church in Ministry* (translated into ten languages) and *Liderazgo y Amistad* (Leadership and Friendship). Presently, he serves as the Executive Presbyter in the General Council of the Assemblies of God, as well as being the first Latino to serve on the national board. He is also the Director of Jesse Miranda Center for Hispanic Leadership.

Mentor and Educator

Miranda founded the Latin American Theological Seminary in the mid-1970s. His main purpose was to facilitate and encourage Hispanic ministers and leaders whom had completed their first level of biblical education into furthering their studies in theology. Ministers and leaders who attend this institution can obtain their bachelor's degree in theology.

Associate Dean at Haggard Graduate School of Theology at Azusa Pacific University

Miranda partnered with Azusa Pacific University in a program that enabled Hispanics leaders to obtain scholarships for their theological studies. Through this endeavor, many Hispanic leaders have been able to obtain a master's degree. As a recipient of this program, I would like to thank Miranda and APU for facilitating the completion of my doctoral degree.

Jesse Miranda Center for Hispanic Leadership at Vanguard University

This is a center dedicated to leadership development and to empower the ministries for service within their own communities. It was through the district's ministry efforts and under Miranda's leadership that the first office building, apartments for retired ministers, and LABI's dorms were constructed.

Hispanic Megachurches in SPLAD

One of SPLAD's leaders and educators by the name of Victor De Leon wrote a magnificent book in 1979, called *The Silent Pentecostals: A Biographical History of the Pentecostal Movement among Hispanics in the Twentieth Century.* In the last section of his book, he made a prediction that can best describe the wonderful growth that Latin American Assemblies of God has experienced. He stated:

> If Jesus tarries in His coming for the church, many changes will take place among the Latin American District churches. Some of the middle-class Hispanic churches will transfer into the

Anglo districts. The Latin American Assemblies of God will continue growing in membership in the areas where the larger segments of Spanish-speaking population are found. As long as the influx of Hispanic people into the United States from Central and South America, Mexico, and the Caribbean continues, the Latin districts will continue to exist. The General Council will take a good look at how they relate to these districts whose leadership will pass from the *second and third generation men to some immigrants* [emphasis added] from other Latin American countries.[6]

Victor De Leon was right. The Assemblies of God's 2014 report lists its 100 largest churches in the United States. Remarkably, out of 12,849 churches, both the first and fifth ranks belong to Hispanic churches within Hispanic districts. New Life Covenant in Chicago (Pastor Rev. Wilfredo de Jesús) ranks **number one** with a membership of 14,620, and Templo Calvario in Santa Ana, California (Pastor Rev. Daniel de León), ranks **number five** with 9,885 members. Also of note are Iglesia Cristiana Misericordia in Laredo, Texas (Pastor Rev. Gilberto Vélez), which ranks number thirty with 3,500 members; Iglesia El Calvario of Orlando (Pastor Dr. Nino Gonzalez), which ranks number thirty one with 3,500 members; and Mission Ebenezer Family Church in Carson, California (Pastor Dr. Isaac Canales), which is number forty-one with a membership of 3,000.[7]
What I find remarkable about these statistics is the fact that most of the leaders of the largest Assemblies of God churches are part of the second and third generation of Hispanic leaders (**two of these churches are part of what used to be SPLAD**). Allow me to share my experiences with some of these leaders. Last year I visited Dr. Isaac Canales's church, Mission Ebenezer Family Church.

He is a second generation leader and a personal friend of mine, who received his M. Div. at the Harvard Divinity School (class of 1978). Dr. Canales was an assistant professor of New Testament Studies and Director of the Hispanic Ministries Department at Fuller Theological Seminary. He also served as President of the historical Latin American Bible Institute (LABI), the first Spanish Pentecostal institute in the Western Hemisphere (founded in 1926).

I am blessed to see how the Lord has given him great wisdom and vision to take a church from a small Hispanic congregation of fifteen people (in 1983) to one of over three thousand. He has purchased a complex that is worth fifteen million dollars in Torrance, California. His church serves the community with multiple worship services in Spanish and English, aimed not only to the first, second, and third generations of Hispanics, but also to Anglos, African Americans, and Asians to say the least.

Rev. Daniel de Leon is the pastor of Templo Calvario in Santa Ana, which is another example of an explosive congregation that was born eighty years ago. My friend, Pastor de Leon, has been a leader and a pastor of this church since 1976, and strongly believes in leadership development. I remember attending his leadership seminars in my early years in ministry. They motivated me to dream big and to get involved in church growth.

THE BIRTH OF THE NORTHERN PACIFIC LATIN AMERICAN DISTRICT

In 1998, under the leadership of Samuel Sanchez as SPLAD's superintendent, the Northern Pacific Latin American District was born in the District Council held in Sacramento, California. NPLAD is a Hispanic Pentecostal District covering two states: the northern part of California, and Nevada. Its first elected superintendent was Rev. Felix Posos. He was a visionary man with a great passion for the Lord and for the emerging generation. He was a graduate from Fuller Theological Seminary, where he received his Masters in Divinity. From the moment he took office until the day of his heavenly departure, his dream for the NPLAD district was that it would harvest more leaders, churches and missions.

It was during his time in office that the district purchased a building in Sacramento, California, where the main offices are now located. NPLAD has been in existence for almost over seventeen years. The second elected superintendent was Rev. Lee Baca, the third one was Rev. Roger Ovalle and the current superintendent elected in 2014 is Rev. Jesse Galindo. He is a second generation Hispanic superintendent. The assistant superintendent is Dr. Raul Sanchez, who belongs to the 1.5 Hispanic generation. The Secretary Treasurer is Dr. Nick Garza, second generation Hispanic.

Demographics

The Northern Pacific Latin American District's territory is subdivided in four regions and fourteen sections within the Northern states of California and Nevada. Region one is located in Sacramento, Stockton, North Central, and Nevada. Region two is in San Francisco, East Bay, Tri-County, and North Coastal. Region three is in San Jose and Salinas. Region four is in Fresno, Tulare, San Joaquin, and Bakersfield.[8] According to the 2014 Assemblies of God U. S. Vital Statistics report, NPLAD currently has 270 credentialed ministers, 172 churches and missions, and approximately 21,640 adherents, with the median age of ministers at 58 years old.[9] The total Hispanic population within California and Nevada is over 14 million.[10]

Ministers by Age

There are three levels of credentials: certified, licensed, and ordained. Out of the 270 ministers, the average age of ordained ministers is 60 years old; licensed ministers 59 years old; and certified ministers 51 years old. The median age for all the ministers is 58[11]. Figure 4 shows that most of NPLAD's ministers are between the ages of 51-60.

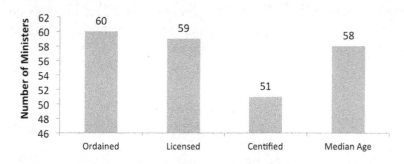

Figure 4. Average ages of NPLAD's ministers.

Hispanic Generations

NPLAD's ministry leadership is comprised of at least four Hispanic "generations." The "first generation" is comprised of the first Latinos that immigrated to the United States. The "1.5 generation" is the Latinos not born in the United States, but brought to the country at a younger age. The "second generation" is the Hispanics born in the United States and the "third generation" is the emerging generation. Although the statistics are not one hundred percent accurate, approximately 50 percent of our credentialed ministers and pastors belong to the first generation of Hispanics; 10 percent to the 1.5 generation; 30 percent to the second generation, and 10 percent to the third generation. Figure 5 shows that the first generation has the highest percentage of credentialed ministers.

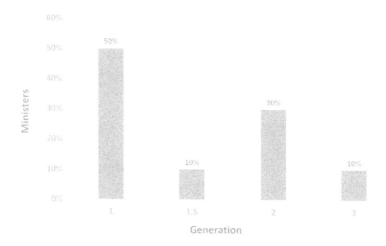

Figure 5. NPLAD's ministers, distribution by generation.

Government

The district has three executive officers: the superintendent, the assistant superintendent, and the secretary treasurer; and two general presbyteries represent the NPLAD district to the Assemblies of God General Council. An executive presbyter governs each region, each of which is subdivided into fourteen sections. Moreover, each of the sections has a sectional presbyter. There is a constitution that governs the district in all of their affairs, and their business sessions.

Doctrine

NPLAD has adopted the Assemblies of God's Statement of Fundamental Truths (16 fundamentals of truth) as the foundation for their distinctive doctrine. In 1916 the Assemblies of God adopted 16 doctrines as a "standard to reach, preach, and teach its people." The Assemblies of God has adopted four of these truths as the "four core beliefs" which are: Salvation, Baptism in the Holy Spirit, Divine Healing, and The Second Coming of Christ.

Philosophy of Ministry

Its main purpose and mission is "to minister to God through worship; ministry to the lost through evangelism; and ministry to the body of Christ through fellowship." These purposes are in their articles of incorporation, which reads:

> The specific purpose of this corporation is to propagate the Gospel of Jesus Christ, according to the Holy Bible, in customs and traditions of Pentecostal Evangelical Christianity, as a church and a convention of churches, and as an administrative agency of and constituent division amenable to The General Council of the Assemblies of God, a Missouri Nonprofit Corporation.
>
> MINISTRY TO THE LORD THROUGH WORSHIP:
> It is the purpose and mission of this District Council to establish and maintain places of worship of Almighty God, our Father, and the Lord Jesus Christ, His only begotten Son, through the Northern Pacific Latin American District Formation

113 Holy Spirit, to conduct business as a church and a convention of churches.

MINISTRY TO THE LOST THROUGH EVANGELISM:
Council through the work of evangelism, under the guidance of the Holy Scriptures to seek and save that which is lost, in both home and foreign fields, in obedience to the command of the Lord Jesus Christ, and in harmony with the teaching and practice of His servants, the Apostles.

MINISTRY TO THE BODY OF CHRIST THROUGH FELLOWSHIP:

It is the purpose and mission of this District Council to build a body of believers in the image of His Son by promoting fellowship with Almighty God and among believers, individuals, and groups, within our churches, and within our larger church community.[12]

Department Ministries

The district is committed to serve and minister to the whole membership and community. To accomplish such commitment, the district has six operating ministries: (a) Christian Education provides assistance and training to Sunday School's teachers; (b) Royal Rangers ministers to the boys aged five and up; (c) Girls' Ministry to the girls aged five and up; (d) Youth ministries to the teenagers, young adults, and single adults; (e) Women's ministries, in charge of ministering to all the district's ladies; and (f) Men's Ministry, which focuses on the all men from our district.

TWENTY-FIRST CENTURY CHALLENGES

God has blessed NPLAD with a leadership that loves the Lord, and a body of ministers that are open to the challenges surrounding their churches and its membership. Although there are various challenges facing our district, I would like to mention five in particular.

Evangelism and New Missions

There are states and regions that are in need of evangelism. The state of Alaska (recently assigned to a new district) is a fertile spiritual ground that has yet to be developed; there are no churches in this area. In my interview with the assistant superintendent Dr. Raul Sanchez, who is in charge of Missions; he expressed the need of more laypeople and ministers willing to answer the call to evangelize and to establish new missions in these regions.[13]

Part-Time Pastors

Not all the churches and especially the missions have a full time pastor. Part of the reason for this situation is the fact that small churches (twenty members or more) and missions (less than twenty members) cannot afford to employ a full-time pastor. Pastors must often have a full- or part-time job in order to make a living while pastoring their respective churches or missions. When this situation takes place, the energy, effectiveness, and time given to the church is affected.

Church Buildings

There are several churches in our regions whose places of worship are not owned by their respective congregations. They must sometimes occupy a storefront facility or a commercial building that does not have adequate accommodations. As a result, pastors and their congregations frequently find themselves without enough financial resources to accommodate the city requirements. This situation is becoming a vital factor for the exodus of the emerging generation; although they love their heritage and their people, they prefer to attend an Anglo congregation whose facilities are more adequate and high-tech.

On the other hand, there are churches that are looking to buy property and when they find it, the lending institutions make it nearly impossible to fund the loan. We also have a few churches that have made enormous sacrifices to own a property; however, due to the economy, they find themselves in great difficulty trying to keep up with the mortgage payments. When both of these situations take place, pastors and their congregations turn to the district office for help. Unfortunately, due to the lack of financial resources, the district encounters heartbreaking situations in their quest to grant their request for financial aid. The Assemblies of God has lending institutions that offers loans to their congregations. Hispanic churches that qualify are welcome to apply. A good number of Hispanic churches have already benefited from this program. However, the churches that do not qualify find themselves in a predicament that is difficult, though not impossible to overcome.

Immigration Status

Some of the first and second generation of Hispanics attending our churches has yet to legalize their immigration status in the United States. We have a group of potential ministers and leaders that can't hold ministerial credentials due to their legal status. As a former pastor of one of the congregations facing this scenario, I can testify to the sadness that one experiences when seeing future leaders or ministers being deported to their countries and forced to leave behind their families and ministry. Adding pain to injury, at times, the pastor and congregation find themselves supporting, consoling, and aiding families that have been left behind, and are now suffering the separation from their parents or spouses due to deportation.

Leadership Development for the Emerging Generation

This is one of the greatest challenge facing our district. The emerging generation is growing by the thousands. Much intentional training is needed in order to produce future leaders. The next and final part of this book will focus on this vital issue.

SUMMARY

In Part C of this book, we have taken a brief look at the history of Latin American Assemblies of God. I have also provided an overview of our NPLAD district's formation, structure, demographics, philosophy of ministry, and challenges. The reader may ask, why the need for a brief history of NPLAD? I humbly believe that in the same way the Lord instructed Moses and Joshua to repeat the story of their miraculous journey from Egypt to the Promised Land (Deuteronomy 4:9-10), it will serve well for our next generation of leaders to become more acquainted with their roots, to better understand where we came from, to appreciate the efforts made by the previous generations, and to read of the wonders that God has done on behalf of the Hispanic Assemblies of God movement.

Part D concentrates on the praxis for effective leadership development among the emerging generation. I give special emphasis to five primary areas encompassing this endeavor, and those are: (a) spiritual formation, (b) discipleship, (c) immigrational leadership outreach, (d) mentoring programs, and (e) the need for a Hispanic Center that can equip the next generation of Hispanic leaders.

STUDY QUESTIONS

1. Where and when was the Northern Pacific Latin American District born?
2. NPLAD's ministry leadership is comprised of at least four Hispanic "generations." Can you name them?
3. What is the median age of all of their ministers between the ages of 51 and 60?
4. What percent of NPLAD's ministers belong to the third or emerging generation?

DISCUSSION QUESTION FOR GROUP STUDY

Each denomination has its challenges and NPLAD is not any different than other denominations. Identify the twenty-first century challenges within your denomination.

CHAPTER PROJECT

Each Hispanic denomination has its own history and humble beginnings. Writing the story of each of them is an important task that everyone should engage in. Assign a group of students or people to do a research corresponding to the beginnings of their respective denomination.

Part D.

Approaches To Leadership

Although some of the past approaches toward leadership are no longer applicable in our present setting, I believe that the principles given by our pioneers have become the cornerstone for the success of many leaders and denominations. Upon my observation, there are at least five areas of leadership that are in need of efficient approaches, and those are: **leadership development, spiritual formation, discipleship, intergenerational outreach, and mentorship, including theological education.** There is a generational gap between the first generation and the emerging generation. This gap does not derive only from age difference, but is also due in part to the dynamics, acculturation, and generational differences among their respective generations. Evidently, we are in need of new approaches in order to close this gap.

The following chapters cover the five approaches as follows: Chapter 7, an example of leadership development taken from my personal life experience; Chapter 8, spiritual formation with an Emerging Hispanic Generation (E.H.G.) context in mind; Chapter 9, a discipleship that is intentional, relational, relevant, and experiential; Chapter 10, effective evangelism that not only has new converts in mind but is also directed toward intergenerational and immigrational groups; Chapter 11, a mentoring program; including a Hispanic theological educational center for leadership development that will prepare our future leaders. I believe that these approaches could also pave the way to a healthy harvest of leadership among the next Hispanic generation; a leadership that could close the existent generational gap and produce new leadership in the years to come.

As a reminder to the reader of this book, my attempt in bringing forward these approaches is not to change the blueprints given to us by our previous generations of Hispanic leaders. Instead, the intention is to suggest updates that can best accommodate the needs of the E.H.G.

Chapter 7

Leadership Development

L eadership development works: it is a vital tool that, when
used properly, can yield a plentiful harvest of new ministers and leaders into God's kingdom. The Greek word used for
leader or to lead is ὁδηγός *hodegos*, which means leader or guide,
but also to lead, to show the way, and to instruct. Leaders have
the responsibility not only to lead but also to develop laypeople
into leaders. The need for more ministers, leaders, and missions
within our Hispanic denominations is undoubtedly evident. If the
population prediction for Hispanics in the year 2060 is accurate,
which would be an estimated 119 million Hispanics; we will face
a shortage of leaders in the coming years. Therefore, the lack of
proper and prompt attention to this particular challenge carries
the peril of losing the next generation of Hispanics leaders in our
denominations. In turn, this could be detrimental and futile, since it
can greatly hinder the future of our Hispanic churches. One of the
answers to these challenges is the formation of a systematic and
intentional leadership development. The aim of this effort should
be to equip the next generation of leaders. Everyone should engage

in this attempt, denomination's officials, pastors, lay leaders and those belonging to the emerging generation.

MY FATHER, AN EXAMPLE OF LEADERSHIP DEVELOPMENT

My father, Matias Morales, was an evangelist, pastor, missionary, and leader with the Assemblies of God for more than seventy years. His first pastoral assignment was to Las Lisas Guatemala, in 1940; his heart was for planting new missions and developing new leaders. In his native country, he opened at least forty missions; those missions became churches that have given birth to hundreds of new missions and churches. What I find remarkable about his ministry is the fact that for every mission he opened, he had a leader ready to take over the new baby church. He was not selfish; his delight was to take the gospel to places that had no evangelical church, and to develop new leaders. Some of the leaders under his ministry became superintendents of the Assemblies of God in Guatemala.

My father was a fearless leader; never afraid of giving his own life for the sake of the gospel. My mother, as well as my older brothers and sisters, witnessed many attempts against his life by people who hated the gospel; however, he never gave up. He kept on preaching until there was no air left in his lungs.

In the early 1970s, and after serving as pastor and missionary for over seven years in Tegucigalpa Honduras, he came to the United States and opened two more missions. One of them is El Sinai, located in Harbor City, CA. (the pastor of this church is my sister Rev. Reyna Morales). Dad was a great leader, and my mother, Silveria, who loved to work with women's ministries, was too. They are my heroes, and they were well-versed in leadership development.

MY LEADERSHIP DEVELOPMENT TRAINING

I was born in church–yes, my delivery into this world took place at the church's parsonage. I did not make it to the hospital. I grew up in church; Dad was the first preacher I heard and the first leader I followed. My first baby steps in ministry, as well as my development into leadership, were under his supervision and mentorship. I am proud to say that I am the fruit of Dad's leadership development. During my younger years in ministry, I was his co-pastor in one of the missions he planted in Harbor City, California, and I was a youth leader in another mission he planted in Echo Park, California (at the Anglo church which was named Bethel Temple). Dad was never afraid to pour out his knowledge, God-given wisdom, and experience upon his children. As a result, we are seven brothers and sisters involved in leadership; six of us are full time in ministry and one is a leader in a local church in California.

My father was not only a leader, but an effective one. As his follower I had confidence in him. He was not only my leader, but more so my friend. We had a great relationship until the day he graduated into heaven. Jesse Miranda, who was also a friend of my father, best describes my dad's type of leadership legacy when he defines a leader as a "principal-friend who lives with integrity in society, practicing intimacy with his followers as Jesus did"[1] in his book, *Liderazgo y Amistad* (Leadership and Friendship). Once again he defines true leadership as one that includes friendship, "The identification of the leader with the people is friendship."[2]

As a Hispanic leader (1.5 generation), I have been working in different leadership capacities among our Hispanic districts. Prior to receiving my first credentials with the Assemblies of God in 1985, I traveled around the country as an evangelist, preaching and teaching in many Hispanic churches. I served as president of the SPLAD's evangelistic association in the 1980's, and from

1999-2012 I worked for NPLAD as a pastor, leader, sectional presbyter, and executive presbyter. I was the senior pastor of a bilingual church called New Dawn Worship Center/Centro de Adoración Nuevo Amanecer in Fremont, California for more than 15 years. Suffice it to say that I became acquainted with the need for leadership development among the next generation through my attendance at numerous leadership meetings and Hispanic district councils, during my visits to various churches, and through conversations with the leadership of different Hispanic denominations. What follows is a compilation of my studies on leadership, which I formed by continual research on this topic, and is also in light of my personal experiences throughout these Hispanic districts.

SUMMARY

Effective Leadership development has its roots on friendship, and in personal relationship.

I thank God for my father, and for the leadership legacy he has left me with. His love for God and his strategies for developing leaders have proved to be effective. Every time I travel to Guatemala, Honduras, and California to give evangelistic crusades, and conferences; I see the results of a man who gave his life to God, ministry, and leadership.

The first generation leaders can best contribute to the E.H.G. by investing time with them. Never underestimate the power of love, friendship, and training, for it may be the most valuable legacy you can leave to the youth that the Lord has entrusted you with.

STUDY QUESTIONS

1. How many missions did Matias Morales open in Guatemala?
2. What was remarkable about Matias Morales regarding his ministry and missions?
3. What generation does the author of this book belong to?

Chapter 8

Spiritual Formation

"My children, with whom I am in labor until Christ is formed in you..." (Galatians 4:19).

Paul understood the importance of spiritual formation. In chapter 4, verse 19 of his letter to the Galatians, he reminded them of their relationship with Christ. The illustration used in this passage is unique since he referred to a mother experiencing labor pains. He alluded to the fact that a baby formed inside the mother's womb has the likeness of the parents when he or she is born. In the same manner, Paul's desire for the Galatians is for Christ to be formed in them; for them to eventually become like Christ. The verb used by Paul in this scripture is μορφόω *morphoō*, and it means "to be formed, in the same nature, in context, be like Christ."[1] Another Greek word related to spiritual formation is μόρφωσις *morphōsis*, meaning "embodiment, essential features, form, or appearance."[2]

What, exactly, is spiritual formation? Spiritual formation is the means by which we can be like Christ. In my personal walk with Christ, I have come to realize that I must allow Christ to be formed in my life. Allow me to give my personal definition of spiritual formation: Spiritual formation is a process by which a follower of Jesus Christ takes on a spiritual journey permitting Christ to be formed in his or her life, eventually resulting in a profound and close intimacy with the Lord.

One of the aims of spiritual formation is the transformation of one's life to reflect our Christian walk with Christ. Clinton states that spiritual formation is the agent which helps us to be Christ-like and to experience God's presence, which eventually empowers us for ministry. He states,

> Spiritual formation refers to development of the inner-life of a person of God, so that the person experiences more of the life of Christ, reflects more Christ-like characteristics in personality and in everyday relationship, and increasingly knows the power and presence of Christ in ministry.[3]

The approach to spiritual formation development should include a clear understanding that this procedure is a **process, not an event**. In other words, it is not something that happens overnight; rather, it is an intentional expedition that should culminate in an intimate relationship with Christ. Spiritual formation encompasses: character development; a clear understanding of what true Christian worship is all about (John 4:23); intentional discipleship; and a systematic study of the word of God.

Spiritual formation is a process not an event. The baptism of the Holy Spirit, and the spiritual gifts mentioned by Paul in his epistles (1 Cor. 12; Eph. 4; Rom. 12), should be used as valuable tools for an effective leadership; however, it is important to point out the proper functionality of the Holy Spirit within the body of Christ. Although the operation of these gifts can serve as a catalyst for spiritual formation, they ought not to be confused with the need to engage in a personal and intimate relationship with the Lord with the aim of becoming Christ-like. Spiritual gifts are important for ministry; they should be the byproduct of a life in total submission to Christ. However, the ultimate goal must be to allow Christ to be formed in us. In the same way, Christian spirituality is the reflection of our spiritual formation; it seeks a life that permeates unity with Christ and is expressed by the way we worship. One of the goals of Christian spirituality is that we ought to seek a deeper relationship with God. Alister E. McGrath in her book *Christian Spirituality* defines Christian spirituality in the following way:

> Spirituality is the outworking in real life of a person's religious faith-what a person does with what they believe. It is not just about ideas, although the basic ideas of the Christian faith are important to Christian spirituality. It is about the way in which Christian faith are important to Christian spirituality. It is about the full apprehension of the reality of God. We could summarize much of this by saying that Christian spirituality is reflection on the whole Christian enterprise of achieving and sustaining a relationship with God, which includes both public worship and private devotion, and the results of these in actual Christian life.[4]

I am in accord with McGrath's definition of Christian spirituality. It is impossible to achieve an intimate relationship with Christ without true worship and without consecrating that life to the Lord. Spiritual formation takes place when we allow the Holy Spirit to work in our lives as He knows how. Allowing the Holy Spirit and His word to guide us, teach us, and take possession of us will result in a transformation into Christlikeness. It is through the Holy Spirit that our mortal bodies receive life; therefore, we no longer live according to the flesh, rather, according to the Spirit (Romans 8:10-13).

Everyone should practice spiritual formation, especially those of us engaged in leadership development. One can be a Hispanic denomination leader, pastor, lay leader, or a member belonging to any Hispanic generations previously mentioned; however, the effectiveness of leadership training should start with our personal relationship with God. Any strategy lacking spiritual formation would prove to be ineffective and unproductive.

The pressure to be a successful leader in a post-*Christendom* world is tangible. Hispanic ministers are experiencing peer pressure from fellow leaders whose primary goals are rooted on church attendance, recognition, or status. Hispanic leaders engaging in leadership development must strive to depart from this mentality and place spiritual formation at the forefront of their next generation training. Furthermore, it should be done with an approach that has the E.H.G. context in mind.

Although spiritual formation encompasses many aspects of Christianity, there is one area that is directly affecting the E.H.G., and that is worship.

CHRISTIAN WORSHIP

Christian worship is part of our spiritual formation. It is one of the outmost expressions of humankind toward its Creator. It is perhaps part of our baby steps that culminates in a deeper relationship with the Lord. Ralph Martin, in his book, *The Worship of God*, quotes Karl Bath's meaning of worship as one of the most exceptional and wonderful expression of God's creation: "Christian worship is the most momentous, the most urgent, the most glorious action that can take place in human life."[5]

According to the New Unger's Bible Dictionary, the Hebrew and Greek words for worship are, respectively: ...Hebrew word *shaha*; To prostrate especially reflexive, in homage to royalty or God (to "bow down"), to prostrate oneself before another in order to do him honor and reverence (Gen 22:5; etc.). This mode of salutation consisted in falling upon the knees and then touching the forehead to the ground (19:1; 42:6; 48:12; 1 Sam 25:41. The Greek word often used for worship is *proskuneo*: Properly to "kiss the hand to (toward) one," in token of reverence; also by kneeling or prostration to do homage-the word most frequently used in the NT; *sebomai*, to "revere" a deity (Matt. 15:9; Mark 7:7; Acts 18:13; 19:27).[6] Worship is an expression of holiness, intimacy, and total surrender to God. Worship is a noble word. Ralph Martin says:

> The term comes into our modern speech from the Anglo-Saxon weorthscipe. This later developed into wordship. It means to attribute worth to an object...If we may elevate this thought to the realm of divine-human relationships, we have a working definition of the term worship ready-made for us. To worship God is to ascribe to Him supreme worth, for He alone is worthy.[7]

God called His people to dedicate themselves to only worship Him and never worship other gods or images. Martin, says, "The *chief aim of worship* is God himself."[8] We find the theological theme of worship through the Old and New Testament. In its narrative, we find out that true worship is aimed toward God and God alone. God must always be the focus, the center, and the reason for which every believer worships. God shall always be the object and His people the subject. Worship is not an alternative, but rather an absolute. Jesus Himself defined the character of true worship by indicating that the only way to worship Him is in the spirit and in truth. "God is spirit, and those who worship him must worship in spirit and truth" (John 4:24). When we worship, we must always have in mind that God is worthy of worship. Our worship should be joyful, offered out of gratitude, and not be done because we feel obligated or because it is mandated.

Worship in the Old Testament

From the beginning, God has required true worship from His people. Satan was expelled from heaven because he wanted the worship for himself, and not for God (Isaiah 14:12-15). In the book of Genesis, God cursed and threw Cain out of His presence for not worshiping Him in spirit and in truth (Genesis 4:1-16). Abel became the model for true worship. True worship represents a worship that will be acceptable to God and gives Him the best, not the leftovers; a worship that comes from the heart and not from obligation (Genesis 4:2-5).

God chose Israel not only to be His people, but most importantly to be the chosen people who would worship Him. Yahweh took them out of Egypt because they weren't able to worship Him in spirit and in truth. God told Moses to go before Pharaoh with this message: "The LORD, the God of the Hebrews, has sent me to say to you: Let my people go, so that they may worship me in the wilderness" (Exodus 7:16 NIV). One of the Ten Commandments calls for worship to Yahweh and nobody else (Exodus 20:4-6). Worship in the Old Testament was expressed through the altar offerings and sacrifices (Genesis 4:2-5; 22:5), prayer and songs (Exodus 15; Psalm 42:8; 100:2), and with dance (Psalm. 149:3; 150:4).

Worship in the New Testament

The opening pages of the New Testament introduce Jesus as God's chosen servant who will ultimately re-establish worship between God and His chosen people. At the end of the Old Testament epoch there is a silence, perhaps coming from a Yahweh who is broken-hearted due to the indifference and the lack of true worship from His chosen people. However, in the New Testament, God took the form of a man-servant; and in so doing, He re-directed His people and His church back to true worship.

Let us look at the Greek word for worship, *proskuneo*, in the New Testament with the following observations: God remains the main object of worship. Satan failed to be the object of worship in heaven, and his second attempt to make Jesus bow down and worship him also failed. Jesus was aware of the fact that one of His purposes on earth was to draw God's people back to worshipping Yahweh instead of Satan. His encounter with Satan serves as a reminder that worship is to be given to God only: "It is written, 'You shall worship the Lord your God and serve Him only'" (Luke 4:8). Jesus outlined the form of worship that God expects from His people. In His encounter with the Samaritan woman at Jacob's well, He delineated the form of worship that pleases God:

> "Woman," Jesus replied, "believe me, a time is coming when you will worship the Father neither on this mountain nor in Jerusalem. You Samaritans worship what you do not know; we worship what we do know, for salvation is from the Jews. Yet a time is coming and has now come when the true worshipers will worship the Father in the Spirit and in truth, for they are the kind of worshipers the Father seeks. God is spirit, and his worshipers must worship in Spirit and in truth" (John 4:21-24 NIV).

True worship is not limited to a specific temple or place. True worship starts in the heart and is to be given in spirit and in truth. Jesus was the perfect example of worship until death. By dying at the cross, He taught us how to not only worship, but also how to remain faithful through our worship even to the point of death:

"Being found in appearance as a man, He humbled Himself by becoming obedient to the point of death, even death on a cross" (Philippians 2:8,).

The early church followed Jesus's example of worship. Before Jesus ascended to heaven, He instructed His disciples to worship the Father as He had done so (John 17:17-24). Throughout the centuries, the early church has gathered to worship the Lord in temples, homes, catacombs; some have even suffered martyrdom for the sake of worshipping Christ. In Acts 2:42-47, we can observe that the early church worshiped God through its faithfulness to: the doctrine of the Apostles, fellowship with the believers, the breaking of bread (Holy Communion), as well as prayer and praise to God at all times.

The author of the First Apology, Justin Martyr, in his document addressed to the Emperor of Rome, Titus, and August Caesar, dated AD 150, described the form of worship used by the early Christians during the Lord's Day. He stated that, "They gathered on a day called Sunday; they read the scriptures; they send up their prayers; they celebrated the Eucharist; they sang; they praised God; and they collected an offering."[9] This document gives us light as to how the early Christians worshipped. Stephen was one of the first martyrs of the early church. He died worshiping God and seeing God's glory (Acts 7).

We are His creation, we ought to worship Him. Paul, in his epistle to the Philippians, exhorts the believers to worship Christ as the triumphal Lord. He says that, "in the name of Jesus every knee will bow, of those who are in heaven and on earth and under the earth, and that every tongue will confess that Jesus Christ is Lord, to the glory of God the Father" (Philippians 2:10-11,). True worship requires the surrendering of ourselves as a holy sacrifice. "Therefore I urge you, brethren, by the mercies of God, to present your bodies a living and holy sacrifice, acceptable to God, which is your spiritual service of worship" (Romans 12:1). We are created to worship and praise Him and to give him glory (Ephesians 1:6). Martin gives us the reasons why we ought to worship Him; he states, "Because of what God has done for us. He has loved us, saved us, blessed us, kept us–and is still doing, we owe it to Him to offer our tributes of corporate praise and prayer."[10]

Prayer

I have chosen prayer as part of worship within spiritual formation because we tend to forget that we can use the practice of prayer as an effective tool in leadership development. By studying the lives of Bible characters engaged in leadership development, we are able to witness to the fact that their ministerial success preceded a life of intimacy with God through prayer. Prayer is a vital component for spiritual formation. Sadly, I have observed that prayer is decreasing, and for some, it is no longer a foundational factor in the lives of younger generations. The emphasis on prayer should play an important role in our Hispanic denominations. There should be no substitution for prayer. In Exodus 33:7-11, we learned that Moses used to spend long periods of time praying and seeking God. As a result, Joshua learned from Moses that when in leadership, prayer becomes an important factor in our lives.

Jesus, being the son of God, was a man of prayer. He always took time to pray. Not only did He teach His disciples how to pray; but He understood the need to pray at all times. Throughout the whole chapter of John 17, Jesus is uttering an intercessory prayer on behalf of His disciples. Jesus prayed to His father not out of necessity, but rather because He loved His father. If we really love the Lord, then we should seek Him through prayer. Regarding God and our love for Him, which is manifested through prayer, Richard Forster, in his book *Prayer*, says, "And overwhelming love invites a response. Loving is the syntax of prayer…Real prayer comes not from gritting our teeth but from falling in love."[11]

What is prayer? Prayer is communication between the human and the divine, between the Creator and His creation; prayer is seeking union with God; therefore, one cannot obtain such union unless one is willing to enter into a journey of prayer. The Greek word used for prayer is *proseuxomai*, pros, meaning "towards, exchange" and *euxomai*, "to wish, pray." Prayer is by far an essential component for spiritual formation. This practice is not new, it has its roots in the Bible, and is in the Old Testament as well as the New Testament. The first chapters of the book of Genesis narrates the creation of humankind and the union between God and His creation. We were created according to His image, "God created man in His own image, in the image of God He created him, male and female He created them" (Genesis 1:27). In the New Testament, we find Jesus instructing His disciples to abide in Him and to be in union with Him.

This union with God, or seeking of God, is not about prayer in itself. It is not about another practice that can make us feel good or accepted by God. In fact, seeking God is about allowing His presence to dwell inside of us, as well as giving God the opportunity to show us His grace and His love. It is a mutual journey by which we not only seek Him, but we can also allow God to find us. To better illustrate the need of prayer as a way to gain intimacy and abiding with Jesus, I will analyze the passage of the vine and the branches found in John 15.

John 15: An Example of Abiding in God

> I am the vine, you are the branches; he who abides in Me and I in him, he bears much fruit, for apart from Me you can do nothing. If anyone does not abide in Me, he is thrown away as a branch and

dries up; and they gather them, and cast them into the fire and they are burned. If you abide in Me, and My words abide in you, ask whatever you wish, and it will be done for you (John 15:5-7).

One of the outcomes of prayer is Christlikeness; it is a way by which we become dependent on Him. John 15 teaches three important elements about spiritual formation: abiding in Christ, fruit-bearing, and obedience (vv.1-17). **Abiding.** This chapter describes a relationship with Christ that we can obtain by abiding with Jesus as the true vine. God the father is the vine grower, and we are the branches. By abiding in Christ we obtain oneness and union with Him. We become friends of God. Through this union, we can experience joy, peace and a relationship with Him.

A person that has experienced oneness with God is a person that has "some understanding of who God is, who has an interactive prayer life with God and finds the joy of God to be natural." **Fruit-Bearing.** This is the result of our oneness with God. A person that bears much fruit is the one whose character has been changed; thus becoming full of love, joy, peace, patience, kindness, goodness, meekness, gentleness & self-control (Galatians 5:22-23). **Obedience.** This is the other benefit of abiding in Christ. By abiding in Him we can bear much fruit; this is manifested in obedience to His commands and by having a loving behavior (vv.10, 12-14, 17). The person who has experienced union with God and is bearing fruit is the one who will have no problem following God's word and His commandments, and who will have a heart full of love, truth, patience, and kindness toward others.

Intercessory Prayer

Abiding in Christ keeps me in continual conversation with Him; allowing me to wait upon the Lord. He will give me whatever

I ask, but while this happens, I pray and wait for God's time and not mine. Intercessory prayer is not given to manipulate or control, but rather to allow my soul to be formed according to His will. This prayer is not lower than the other forms of prayer, it helps to develop a Christ-like character. The Lord has given us the freedom to ask and as we ask, we engage in our journey of seeking His face (Psalm 27:8). This practice develops a character full of love and compassion toward people in need. It also reminds us of the importance to pray for others in need. I will never forget my experience during class when I wept while praying for a person whom the Holy Spirit had placed in my heart to pray for. This practice turned out to be not only an intercessory prayer but also a weeping prayer.

Jesus Christ practiced intercessory prayer. He prayed for Peter and for his faith not to fail: "Simon, Simon, behold, Satan has demanded permission to sift you like wheat; but I have prayed for you, that your faith may not fail; and you, when once you have turned again, strengthen your brothers" (Luke 22:31-32). The emerging generation ought to seek union with the Lord in prayer, intercede for their leaders and communities, and make prayer part of their daily schedule.

I conclude with a prayer that has become part of my meditation with God. The reading of this prayer pervades union with God and infuses a deep desire to abide in Christ at all times. This prayer opens anybody's heart for transformation, it speaks about Christ being with me, inside of me, and all over me. One of the stanzas of this prayer, "Breastplate of St. Patrick," reads,

> Christ be with me, Christ within me,
> Christ behind me, Christ before me,
> Christ besides me, Christ to win me,
> Christ to comfort me and restore me,
> Christ beneath me, Christ above me,
> Christ in quiet, Christ in danger,
> Christ in heart of all that love me,

Christ in mouth of friends and strangers.[12]

One may ask, "Does spiritual formation have anything to do with prayer?" or, "Is it proper to assume that this practice can be used as a strategy for Hispanic leadership development?" The answer to both questions is a resounding "YES!" As a Hispanic leader I can testify to the fact that prayer is important, and that we have failed to teach our next generation of Hispanics the importance of dedicating quality time with God. We have viewed this practice as obsolete and old-fashioned, finding place only in our patristic period (first centuries in the history of the church, 100-451 A.D.); however, as never before, our new generation is in need of learning the discipline of prayer in order to gain intimacy with God.

Although programs, events, and crash conferences aimed to train our next generation can be beneficial, depriving them from the spiritual benefits found in the practice of prayer could prove to be detrimental to their spiritual formation. Leadership development training for future leaders must include prayer as part of the spiritual formation. One of the purposes of our quick assessment on the theology of worship is to bring more biblical light and comprehension among the myriad of misconceptions and confusion regarding Hispanic liturgy, or public worship in our present time. The Hispanic praxis of public worship has been the object of debates, wrongful application, legalism, and at times, divisions among Hispanic generations. **Our present leadership owes the E.H.G. a theological and practical delineation of what true worship is all about.** Failing to do so could damage the already fragmented theology of worship that our next generation has currently inherited. In the next segment of this chapter, I will deal with the conflicts and challenges facing the E.H.G. when it comes to public worship.

WORSHIP CONFLICTS BETWEEN THE E.H.G. AND THE HISPANIC CHURCHES

In our previous segment, I outlined the elements of worship practiced by the early church during the Lord's Day (Sunday), which are: scripture reading, prayer, the participation of the Eucharist, singing, praising, and offering. This document helps us to defuse the misconception that public worship is limited to music or prayer. We should view what takes place in a Christian worship service as part of our worship unto God. Public worship typically takes place inside a sanctuary, but the scope of true worship speaks of a lifestyle chosen by a follower of Jesus Christ. In what follows, I will concentrate on the conflicts and challenges taking place at a Hispanic worship service.

Language

Nowadays it is not unusual to see the generational diversity among Hispanics in a typical Sunday morning worship service. I will venture to say that according to my observations during years of ministry among Hispanic churches, in each service you can count on at least three generations of worshippers. The first generation insists on a worship service that is strictly in the Spanish language. Their argument is that the E.H.G. needs to assimilate the Spanish culture and language. Although part of their argument could be correct, the reality of it is entirely different. The effects of this practice have created a problem of mammoth ramifications that we must address.

It has been my personal observation concerning the emerging generation that as they are growing up, they attend and worship in a Hispanic church with a Spanish worship service only. However, as soon as they have a chance, they migrate to non-Hispanic congregation that is willing to offer them a worship experience in their own language. This is due to the fact that we have failed to realize that, though their last name is Hispanic, Spanish may not be their preferred or main language. Although the emerging generation may understand the Spanish spoken at home; that does not mean they speak fluently in Spanish. If you do not believe this reality, try placing a first generation Hispanic person in an English service and then tell me how much they have assimilated or enjoyed it? The biggest excuse one can give the E.H.G. as we force them to our mode is "you need to learn how to speak Spanish."

Holland quotes Grebler, Moore, and Guzman's four stages of Acculturation/ Language Variables. He says that the Hispanic generation is constantly undergoing "stage one, Spanish only; stage two, Spanish and some English; stage three, bilingual/bicultural; stage four, English only."[13] He calls this the "Upward Social Mobility."[14] Most of the E.H.G. generation is in-between the third stage and heading towards the fourth one. The problem is, that if we insist on having Spanish-only worship services, there is a possibility that when it is time for the emerging generation to go to college, we may as well **kiss them good bye**, because more than likely, they will not return to our churches. We may never have them back as active members in our Hispanic Spanish-speaking-only congregations.

Suggested Approaches

The need for at least a **bilingual worship** service is imminent. One can't continue with the Spanish-only mentality with the hope that our emerging generation will adjust. In reality, those congregations that have already made the adjustment will continue to welcome those we have neglected. Anglo churches are receiving our E.H.G. youth in great numbers. This particular group is coming back from college as professionals, trained and eager to serve; but sadly, they often don't return to our Hispanic churches.

Lastly, we as a Hispanic denomination should not be afraid of nurturing and supporting congregations that have moved to an English-only format. If the makeup of their churches is comprised of E.H.G., so be it; let them operate in their own style and language. Let us embrace them and encourage them instead of criticizing them for their efforts. The trend is changing. I know of great Hispanic Churches offering Spanish services for the first generation and English service for the second and subsequent generations. Two of these churches are among the top 100 churches in attendance within the Assemblies of God movement, surpassing the non-Hispanics district churches.[15]

Music Style

The first generation of pastors and leaders continue to have worship services with songs sung by their great-great grandfathers. This may be an exaggeration, but the fact of the matter is, that although the music style is good, harmonious, inspiring, and uplifting, it is not appealing to the E.H.G. anymore. This can be evident when attending a youth Hispanic convention. Though they may hear some of the hymns sung by our generation, for the most part, they have their own style of music and dread sitting in pews singing the good, old-fashioned songs in Spanish.

I personally enjoy singing those songs, since I grew up with them, but in reality, the E.H.G. is seeking a music style relevant to its generation. It is not unusual to hear complaints from the first generation members when exposed to the contemporary music program. For example, a precious first generation lady attended a service conducted by the young people in her church. At the beginning of the music program, to her surprise, they turned on the smoke machine. Her first expression inside the sanctuary was "ese humo es del diablo!" (that smoke is of the devil).

Suggested Approaches

The leader, pastor, or music director ought to be open to **new styles** of music and programs. They need to allow the E.H.G. to get involved in the planning of the music program. One suggestion for this is to try mixing programs that include the old with the new songs. I believe that the E.H.G. needs to experience our music heritage, but not in a way that forces a program that is neither in their own language nor in their own context.

Church Building

Some of our Hispanic churches don't own the buildings where they worship. Pastors find themselves with no other alternative than to rent facilities that are not suitable for worship. The location, the high rent, and any additional challenges they face oftentimes affect the quality or presentation they can offer to their church membership. The group of Hispanic churches owning their own facilities find themselves at the crossroads as they embark in a much needed remodeling that will make their building more appealing to the younger generation.

For the most part, the first generation of membership has no problem attending any building, any place at any time, but not so for the E.H.G. They are used to high-tech buildings at school, work, or colleges during weekdays. Coming back to worship in a building that is inadequate or old is a challenge to say the least. Currently the lack of financial resources is having a gigantic impact in some of our churches and even our Hispanic denominations. Pastors who are engaging in a building fund drive, with the goal of building a new facility or remodeling their existing one, are having great difficulties finding institutions to fund their projects.

Adding pain to injury, the economy, the loss of jobs, and the low income levels of some of their members makes it hard or even impossible to qualify for a loan. Some of the Christian financial institutions are even turning down Hispanic churches applying for a loan because they do not qualify. What should they do? How can they obtain their financial needs? Their heart is in the right place, but their resources are limited. Because of the aforementioned dilemma, our E.H.G. are migrating to churches whose facilities are more adequate and appealing to them. In the past, most of the Anglo sister churches were opening their doors to our Hispanic congregations who were in need of a building to worship. Sadly, the doors are slowly closing, and a new trend is taking place, which is the opening of Spanish departments among Anglo churches.

The problem with this trend is the fact that the Hispanic congregation, who attend or accept this proposal, are often finding themselves under an administration or leadership of pastors and leaders who do not understand the Hispanic context. Thus, the Hispanic congregation, not only have to undergo their supervision, but most notably, they find it hard to operate independently. Although there may be successful cases, sometimes the result of these joint efforts is the loss of the E.H.G. members who prefer attending the English congregation instead of supporting the Hispanic one. Some of the Hispanic congregations are asked to join the English congregation in their worship service instead of facilitating an adequate place of worship for them.

With regards to the acculturation dilemma, Holland's writings confirms the exodus of the E.H.G. population who are choosing to disassociate with their roots, he states "highly acculturated middle-class Hispanic Americans, who are comfortably bilingual or fluent only in English, tend to associate only with Anglo churches, while having little to do with ministry among the Spanish-speaking population.[16]

I remember back in the 1970s when someone asked my father to open up a new mission in Los Angeles within an Anglo sister church. At the beginning, we were given the living room of a house that belonged to the church to conduct our services. Once the congregation grew to approximately one hundred people, we were offered the basement of the church with the condition that we had to join the English congregation in their Sunday morning worship. The problem with this proposal was the fact that their congregation consisted of a handful of senior citizens whose worship style was totally different than ours. Without much success, my father tried to explain the need for independent growth. He offered to participate in united services at least once a month in order to have fellowship and to partake of the Holy Communion together. Sadly, they denied his offer. They dismissed him as a pastor, and the Hispanic mission we worked so hard to establish came to an end.

A few years ago, I learned that when the Anglo church where we opened the mission closed its doors, and it donated its building to an inner-city Anglo ministry. When this ministry outgrew the place, they purchased a bigger building, and sold the previous one to a Hispanic ministry.

I am grateful to the Anglo ministers and churches that in the past have allowed the Hispanic churches to use their facilities without an association restrictions or reservations; I am also appreciative to those congregations that have not forced the Hispanic missions to become departments of their congregations; but rather, have worked together to aid and to facilitate the growth of Hispanic missions. I know of some cases where the Anglo churches, including Anglo denominations have aided a Hispanic new mission to buy a building or have sold theirs at a great discounted price. In other cases they have donated their building, or helped them to build their own. This is extremely important since some of these congregations, at the beginning of their ministry, find it hard to get established.

I don't know if the approach of becoming an Anglo department will harvest a new generation of Hispanic leaders. I would like to see us working together and helping one another. We can achieve this goal if Anglo church leaders and pastors offer their help to Hispanics' new missions by allowing us to operate independently and within our own context.

I understand that there are some Hispanic leaders that need to learn how to respect, care, and administrate a building that is not theirs. I am also aware of some cases where there is a mutual agreement, fellowship, and association between an Anglo church and a Hispanic new mission. The association has worked wonderfully, yielding a great harvest for God's kingdom. However, these cases are unique and often require an Anglo church with a big heart for Hispanic missions, an open mind and willingness to understand the Hispanic culture, and a leadership that is willing to work together without taking advantage of each other.

New Approaches

The need to engage in healthy conversation with our Anglo denomination's leaders is imperative. It is only through discussing these issues with an open mind that we will be able to work together and to help one another. They have the buildings and the resources, while we have the passion to open new missions and to see more of our Hispanics people being saved. I believe that we can work independently, yet in unity we can grow together within our own distinctive contexts. This analysis seeks to better understand the challenges that our Hispanic churches are facing instead of what could be wrongly interpreted as a direct attack against the Anglo church as a whole. I am grateful for their efforts and contributions to the formation of our denominations, and churches; however, the urgency of the matter before us requires sincerity, openness, maturity, and understanding.

It will not do justice to this dilemma if I do not mention the fact that we ought to do our part also. Oftentimes, as Hispanics, we have the tendency to blame someone else for our shortcomings. We need to encourage our next generation to study, go to college, prepare themselves in their careers, and to be committed to their Hispanic congregations.

Once they become professionals, they will be able to invest their talents and financial resources in our districts and churches only if we help them to develop their leadership skills in their own context. Ortiz addresses the need for our generation to understand the emerging generation by giving them the freedom to declare their educational dynamics. He says, "Second generation Hispanics must be understood anthropologically and sociologically, so that the church can provide 'room' for them to express their cultural dynamics."[17]

Our generation ought to seek wisdom, guidance, and mentoring in the area of finances. We need proper stewardship amid the Hispanic leadership as well as budget planning, building planning, and appropriate accounting procedures. The Hispanic church's membership must receive training and motivation to plant a financial seed in God's kingdom that would eventually produce good dividends. If we pray and do our part, we can expect the Lord to do His, and God will provide miracles that will facilitate the expansion of His kingdom on earth as well as suitable and adequate facilities for the generations to come.

Providing a proper place for worship, and doing so in a context that will welcome the emerging generation, is essential. They need to be welcomed, otherwise they will continue to exit our churches as well as their Christian bedrock. The recent statistics on the Millennials' religious affiliations is alarming. Pew research reports the following concerning this issue:

> Our new survey of U.S. Hispanics and religion enables us to take a more detailed look at whether the trend holds true among the country's largest

ethnic minority. And indeed, Hispanic Millennials mirror young American adults overall in their lower rates of religious affiliation and commitment compared with their older counterparts. Similar shares of Hispanic Millennials (28%) and U.S. Millennials overall (31%) say they have no particular religion or are atheist or agnostic. By comparison, the percentages of Hispanic adults overall and American adults overall who are religiously unaffiliated are lower (18% of Hispanics, 20% of all U.S. adults).[18]

STORIES OF SUCCESSFUL EMERGING GENERATION CHURCHES

I would like to share the story of a third generation leader who perhaps fits the profile of an effective leader that has embraced the aforementioned changes with unprecedented results. His name is Carlos Ramos; he is a fourth generation Hispanic. The name of his church is Refuge Church/Templo Refugio, and it is located in Fort Worth, Texas. In 2004 he took over a church that for the most part had a first generation membership. Although the church has gone through a long period of adjustments, I am happy to report that a few years ago his church transitioned to a church with two services; one in English and the other in Spanish. The church has grown from an attendance of 70 people to 700. Just a few weeks ago, they added a third service, and are now holding two services in English and one in Spanish. The church has invested thousands of dollars to purchase and remodel a larger building, in order to accommodate the needs of the emerging generation. I have personally met Pastor Ramos, and I consider him not only my friend, but also a great husband and a father. His emerging generation children are involved in church, and they enjoy serving the Lord. I always say that "**I don't want to pastor a church where my**

own children cannot belong, will not belong, or feel like they don't belong." Rev. Ramos is also a great third generation leader who is leading the way to a prosperous emerging generation leadership development within the Hispanics. There are other churches that are doing a remarkable job with second and third generation leaders. My late cousin Benjamin Paredes pastored a church named Templo Betania. It began with a little over 100 people, and by the time Benjamin went home to be with the Lord in 2012, the church had an attendance of over 1,500 people. His wife Maribel Paredes is the current pastor, and one of his sons, Benji (a second generation leader), is the assistant pastor.

SUMMARY

After all is said and done, our love for the Lord should reflect our desire to engage in a personal relationship with Him. Robin Mass and Gabriel O'Donnell in their book *Spiritual Traditions for the Contemporary Church* could have not said it better with their words,

> Our experience must be tested in the light of reasoned reflection on Scripture, history, and the teaching of the Church and the communal confession of the Church's faith must be lived out by each of us in a personal love relationship with God.[19]

We have taken a quick view of what spiritual formation is all about, with special emphasis on worship and its challenges for leadership development among Hispanic churches. Next, we will discuss the importance of discipleship as an approach to leadership.

STUDY QUESTIONS

1. What is the Greek root word for "formation," used by Paul in Galatians 4:19, and what is the definition of this word?
2. What is the meaning of the word "worship" according to Karl Bath and quoted by Ralph Martin?
3. What type of worship service (in terms of language) is at least needed amongst our emerging generation?
4. The leader, pastor, or music director ought to be open to what styles of music and programs?
5. What type of building facilities are the emerging generation used to at school, work, or college during the week?

DISCUSSION QUESTION FOR GROUP STUDY

Allow your group to discuss the styles of music used in their worship services. Is your church or denomination including the emerging generation in their worship service program? If not, allow the group that is including the emerging generation to give suggestions to those that are not.

CHAPTER PROJECT

Some of our Hispanic churches don't own the buildings where they worship. Pastors find themselves with no other alternative than to rent facilities that are not suitable for worship. Assign a group of people to do a research identifying the challenges facing their denominations with regards to church buildings, and come up with possible solutions.

Chapter 9

Discipleship

I t was an early morning and I had just finished an evangelistic crusade. Upon arriving home, I turned on my answering
machine and heard a message that pierced my heart. It was one
of my friends, whom I had known for many years. He told me,
"Maynor, my son is dead–my son is dead! They found him dead in
the middle of a park." I may never know the cause of Peter's death,
but one thing I do know: Peter was playing church. He tried hard
to stay away from some friends who eventually pulled him away
from following Christ. Peter's ventures away from the Lord led
him to stray from the church he once knew, attended, and was committed to. Although he tried many times to come back to church,
his efforts were unsuccessful; he could not find the courage and
strength to stay away from people who did not fear the Lord. He
wandered back and forth through the revolving door of the church
until the day he died.

Peter was one of my closest friends, and his father, who was a
well-respected pastor and recognized leader in Los Angeles, was
also my friend. Peter's father asked me to be the speaker at his
son's funeral. It was hard to deliver the message, knowing that in

front of me was the body of a personal friend. After delivering the message, I made an altar call, and to my surprise, more than one hundred young people came forward to recommit their lives to the Lord. At the end of the funeral service, Peter's father told me two things that I will never forget as long as a live. First he said, "Maynor, one of the hardest things for a pastor is to see his own son die the way my son died, alone at the park." The second thing he said was, "All the young people that came forward were once members of this church. They were once serving the Lord; sadly, they left the church and went back into the world."

On my way back home, I could no longer hold my tears, not only because I missed Peter, but more so because though I did my best to help him, encourage him, and uplift him, I felt that I somehow failed him. My thoughts drifted back, reliving the events that took place during our friendship. In the end, I came to the conclusion that Peter and the other youths who came to the altar failed to embraced one foundational area in their lives: to be a true follower of Jesus.

I often wonder how many young people are waiting to be discipled, or perhaps how many have been wrongly discipled. Discipleship is foundational factor of effective leadership development. Without a discipleship, a leader will receive a crippled ministerial formation. If spiritual formation aims a Christ-like character and attitude, discipleship aims towards the proper preparation for action in ministry. It relates to the beginning steps taken by a Christian under the direction of a leader that would eventually culminate in maturity and service in the Lord's kingdom.

WHAT IS DISCIPLESHIP?

Then Jesus came to them and said, "All authority in heaven and on earth has been given to me. Therefore go and make disciples of all nations,

baptizing them in the name of the Father and of
the Son and of the Holy Spirit, and teaching them
to obey everything I have commanded you. And
surely I am with you always, to the very end of the
age" (Matthew 28:18-20 NIV).

Before our Lord Jesus Christ ascended to heaven, He gathered his disciples and gave them one of the most essential, fundamental, and exceptional commission known to Christians. That commission was to go and make disciples. As He commissioned them, He released God's authority into their lives. In so doing, Jesus **empowered** them to make disciples, to further baptize, and to teach. The Lord's command to make disciples left no room for options; it only left room for obedience.

As we survey the gospels, especially in the book of Acts, we find the followers of Christ engaging in discipleship. They took their task so seriously that nothing, not even death, could stop them from carrying out the Lord's commands. As Christians, we can testify to the fact that the work done by Jesus's disciples has been crowned by the multiplication of disciples all around the world, including the Hispanics within the United States.

What was the Lord trying to get across to His disciples for more than three years? The word disciple comes from the Greek word μαθητεύω *mathēteuō*, and it means both to teach and to instruct (as in to make a disciple), and to be a disciple. Those who are willing to be discipled are called μαθητής or *mathētēs* meaning a learner, a pupil.[1] According to Matthew 28:19, the task given to the disciples was to go and find learners or pupils for the Lord's kingdom, and to impart what they had received directly from the Lord unto others.

To better understand the meaning and the magnitude of being a disciple, it is important to go back in history and to study the way Jewish people viewed discipleship. In Jesus's times, before you could train learners or pupils you had to become a rabbi. A rabbi was a Jewish teacher or a scholar. To be a disciple under a rabbi was not an easy task. First, they asked you to study and to memorize the Torah. After further studies and memorization of Jewish history and literature, you had to find a rabbi who was willing to take you under his wing. Before a rabbi could agree to train you, he would test your knowledge and integrity to see if you qualified to be his disciple. Upon passing such tests, the rabbi would say to you, "come and follow me," and from that moment on he called you his apprentice.

The true meaning of the word disciple goes beyond being a follower, learner or a pupil (*mathētēs*). It is the idea of a willingness to receive a training that will cause a change of mind, heart, and goals. The main goal of discipleship was to be willing to have a personal relationship with your rabbi that would eventually culminate in oneness between the teacher and the disciple, the rabbi and the pupil; to put it in other words, to "become" a teacher or rabbi. When Jesus told His disciples "come follow Me" (Mark 1:17-20), He was implying the following: "I am extending an invitation to you to be a part of My kingdom; however, if you decide to accept My invitation, it will require major changes in the way you think and act to say the least. I cannot settle for anything less than your acceptance to enter into a divine covenant, an intimate relationship with Me. You will follow Me (leave your families and business behind), you will learn from Me, and you will be My pupil; Where I go, you will go, where I sleep you will sleep, what I eat, you will eat, and the way I suffer you will suffer too (including death via martyr); you will know Me, and I will reveal My kingdom to you. At the end, you will be promoted to be an apostle (*apostolē*), you will be sent to the world to extend My kingdom, empowered (*energeō, energēma, exousia, dúnamis*) to preach (*kerygma*) the gospel (*euaggelion*), to make disciples (*mathētēs*), and to send them out (*apostolē*), just as I have done with you". In my personal observation, **that is what leadership development is all about.**

When Jesus called His disciples to follow Him (Matthew 4:18-22), most of them, if not all, felt unworthy and unqualified, yet they felt privileged to follow Jesus and to be His apprentice. This is what the kingdom of God is all about: the ministry of Jesus was about proclamation, demonstration, and teaching. Keith J. Matthews says the following regarding discipleship, "Once we enter the kingdom of God, we must then learn how to live in it. We must be willing to become Jesus's apprentices, for a disciple is an apprentice."[2] It is impossible to call ourselves Christians if we are not willing to first become His apprentices and submit to His apprenticeship. The twelve disciples were very much aware of the calling when they first signed up. Although they felt unqualified at the beginning of their apprenticeship with Jesus, at the end they became true followers of Jesus, even to the point of giving their lives for the sake of the Lord's kingdom.

Unfortunately, throughout the years, Christians have forgotten the Lord's command of discipleship. Instead, discipleship has become something optional. We are too busy trying to get our churches filled to capacity at the expense of sacrificing true discipleship. Fancy programs, Hollywood-style Christian productions, buildings, and even so-called Christian celebrities have replaced true discipleship. The Lord's great commission has become, as Willard says "the great omission." Substituting the great commission for the "great omission" has the potential of hurting the harvest of our next generation. Dallas Willard writes about the danger of discipleship omission in his book, *The Great Omission*: "The greater issues facing the world today with all its heart-breaking needs is whether those who by profession as culture are identified as 'Christians' will become disciples-students, apprentices, practitioners of Jesus Christ."[3]

For those who are seeking true discipleship, one must accept God's salvation by grace and through his son Jesus Christ. In the primitive church, the first group of converts repented from their sins, and then, soon after, became followers and apprentices. The second chapter of the book of Acts records this magnificent event that took place shortly after Peter's preaching at Pentecost, which eventually harvested future disciples:

> With many other words he warned them; and he pleaded with them, "Save yourselves from this corrupt generation." Those who accepted his message were baptized, and about three thousand were added to their number that day. They devoted themselves to the apostles' teaching and to the fellowship, to the breaking of bread and to prayer (Acts 2:40-42 NIV).

One of the problems among some Pentecostal Hispanic churches is the tendency to put more emphasis on the forgiveness of sin and less or none on discipleship. For others it is putting more emphasis on social issues, and less or none on discipleship. Dallas, in his book T*he Divine Conspiracy,* writes about this situation, which he calls the "gospel of sin management." He says,

> When we examine the broad spectrum of Christian proclamation and practice, we see that the only thing made essential on the right wing of theology is forgiveness of the individual's sin. On the left it is removal of social or structural evils. The current gospel then becomes a 'gospel of sin management.' Transformation of life and character is no part of the redemptive message.[4]

155

Thus, I believe that we must apply a proper balance. On one hand, we cannot ignore the importance of salvation, since without it, how could we acquire candidates for discipleship? On the other hand, we cannot assume that one no longer needs discipleship once one is saved. Moreover, Willard asserts that believing in this methodology can give the "impression that it is quite reasonable to be a "vampire Christian."" He goes on to say, "First, there is absolutely nothing in what Jesus himself or his early followers taught that suggests you can decide just to enjoy forgiveness at Jesus's expense and have nothing more to do with him."[5] I could not agree more with Willard's statement. We ought to substitute the "great omission" with a **great discipleship**.

I believe that effective discipleship will harvest a generation of leaders that are appreciative of the redemptive work of Christ and have an understanding that salvation hasn't come cheap. Additionally, there are leaders who are willing to pay the price by signing up to be apprentices of the Lord Jesus Christ. Therefore, discipleship closes the doors to "cheap grace." The well-known German author and theologian Dietrich Bonhoeffer, born in 1906, writes in his book, *The Cost of Discipleship*, the following immortal words regarding cheap grace:

> Cheap grace is the deadly enemy of our Church. We are fighting today for costly grace. Cheap grace means grace sold on the market like cheapjack's wares. The sacraments, the forgiveness of sin, and the consolations of religion are thrown away at cut prices. Grace is represented as the Church's inexhaustible treasury, from which she showers blessings with generous hands, without asking questions or fixing limits…Cheap grace is the preaching of forgiveness without requiring repentance, baptism without the church discipline, Communion

without confession, absolution without personal confession. Cheap grace is grace *without discipleship*, [italics added] grace without the cross, grace without Jesus Christ, living and incarnate... it is the call of Jesus Christ at which the disciple leaves his nets and follows him... Costly grace is the gospel which must be *sought* again and again, the gift which must be *asked* for, the door at which a man must *knock*. Such grace is *costly* because it calls us to follow, and it is *grace* because it calls us to follow *Jesus Christ*.[6]

In my journey as an evangelist, pastor and leader for over thirty-seven years, I have noticed that some pastors, ministers, and even teachers have compromised and watered down the pure commission of discipleship. Discipleship is the answer to "cheap grace," therefore, discipleship should be costly. Furthermore, it takes time, preparation, and a great effort to disciple those who want to be Jesus's apprentices. Since discipleship is foundational for the development of future leaders, it behooves us leaders to engage in the task of discipleship. I used the term discipleship because some leaders do not take this task seriously or incorporate it to the E.H.G. context. The effectiveness of our discipleship training for the next generation rests on the review of what has worked and what is in need of updates or new approaches.

DISCIPLESHIP QUADRANT APPROACH

Allow me to introduce what I call the discipleship quadrant approach. This approach is comprised of four areas of discipleship, which we find in Figure 6 that Jesus practiced with His disciples: (a) intentional discipleship, (b) relational discipleship, (c) relevant discipleship, and (d) experiential discipleship.

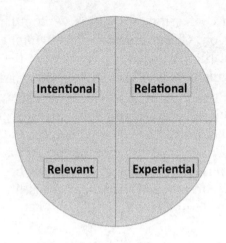

Figure 6. The discipleship quadrant.

Intentional Discipleship

> Now as Jesus was walking by the Sea of Galilee,
> He saw two brothers, Simon who was called Peter,
> and Andrew his brother, casting a net into the sea;
> for they were fishermen...And He said to them,
> "follow Me, and I will make you fishers of men"
> (Matthew 4:18-19).

This passage shows us that the choosing of the disciples was not an accident or a coincidence; instead, Jesus was intentional in His choices. What I mean by intentional is reflected by the fact that the act of choosing disciples was prayed and planned for. The Holy Spirit led Jesus into the wilderness to pray and to fast. In fact, one of His assignments after His forty days of fasting was to choose the men that would eventually receive His discipleship training (Matthew 4:1-19). In my humble opinion, when choosing candidates for discipleship who eventually will become future leaders, one ought to seek the direction of the Holy Spirit through prayer and fasting. It is only then that one can move on and choose those whom the Lord has placed upon your heart to disciple. Notice that the first group of disciples who Jesus called were fishermen. One would think, "What a way to start!" However, history would prove that although they were simple people, they made a choice to follow Him and eventually became effective "fishers of men."

A. B. Bruce, the author of the classic nineteenth century book *The Training of The Twelve*, best describes the awesome privilege of being chosen as Jesus's apprentice and witness. He states:

> That some of the apostles were comparatively obscure, inferior men cannot be denied; but even the obscurest of them may have been most useful as witnesses for Him with whom they had companied from the beginning. It does not take a great man to make a good witness, and to be witnesses of Christian facts was the main business of the apostles.[7]

Moreover, if we allow the Spirit to lead us, the characteristics of those who will be chosen make no difference. I believe that if we do our part, the Lord will do His. Clinton states that the process of leadership selection "is a major function of all Biblical leadership." He goes on to say that "leadership selection refers to the human side of recognizing potential for leadership."[8]

We need to understand intentional discipleship as an opportunity to develop future leaders. They will undergo different phases throughout their journey; however, with the help of the leader they will be successful every single step of the way. Robert Clinton in his work, *The Making of a Leader*, writes about six phases that the leader in training will have to undergo:

Phase one: Sovereign Foundations
Phase two: Inner-Life Growth
Phase three: Ministry Maturing
Phase four: Life Maturing
Phase five: Convergence
Phase six: Afterglow[9]

Clinton states that each of these phases "is a unit of time in a person's life."[10] Moreover, these phases will require a leader who is willing not just to choose, but to lead, guide and support his disciples. One of the problems I see among some Hispanic leaders is a lack of desire to disciple others. The second problem is a lack of wisdom, thus they often reflect prejudice when choosing apprentices. When it comes to discipleship, our Hispanic mentality needs to shift from **accidental to intentional**. The omission of discipleship is definitely hurting the development of our E.H.G. Although discipleship training has its risks, and failures, it is full of rewards and successes. Some Hispanic leaders do not disciple others because they are afraid of failure or are fearful that the person they are training may eventually take over their leadership position. Additionally, others might choose to exercise prejudice by relying on their own instincts, likings, and preferences, instead of seeking the Lord's guidance. If God has called you, your job is not to worry about your own position, but rather to make disciples and to advance God's kingdom on earth.

Allow me to elucidate on one of my own personal examples. I remember when I first came to the United States many years ago. The pastor of the church that I congregated was dynamic leader; he was a good preacher; a man of prayer; true worshipper; and a good administrator. By the time he died, he left a big congregation with a fully-purchased church building and a substantial amount of money in the church's savings account. However, in my humble opinion, there was one area that I wish he had exercised and emphasized, and that area is intentional discipleship. It was only by the grace of God that a good number of us, the former emerging generation, found our way to ministry. That is one of the reasons that has compelled me to embraced discipleship as one of my main priorities.

There are many apprentices waiting to be selected to take on the journey of discipleship. While we allow other issues that we think are important to occupy us, they should not take the place of intentional discipleship. Our next generation is counting on leaders who are willing to take a risk to embark in the arduous yet rewarding task of intentional discipleship.

Relational Discipleship

Have you ever wondered why Jesus did not ask the disciples if they **wanted** to follow Him? We know that some of them were disciples of John (John 1:37), but I believe that there is more to it. Jesus did not ask but **told** them to "follow Me." History will witness to the fact that, at least for the next three years, Jesus was inviting them into a mutual relationship. We understand that in those days, as previously stated, that the rabbi was the one who did the choosing. The disciples probably didn't feel worthy of such an honor; yet, they couldn't disregard the great opportunity to be trained by Jesus. They were also aware of the fact that in those days, those considered to be trainees were asked to move in with their rabbis.

If the meaning of the term rabbi is a teacher or a leader, then, one of my observations in this proposition made by Jesus was: if you follow Me, I will give you My word that I will personally have fellowship with you and I will train you for the next three years how to be My disciples for life. One of Jesus's disciples, John, testified of the relationship that Jesus had with His disciples. He writes "And the Word became flesh, and dwelt among us, and we saw His glory, glory as of the only begotten from the Father, full of grace and truth" (John 1:14). Later on, John passed on what he had personally experienced from his Rabbi. He says:

> What was from the beginning, what we have heard, what we have seen with our eyes, what we have looked at and touched with our hands, concerning the Word of Life-and the life was manifested, and we have seen and testify and proclaim to you the eternal life, which was with the Father and was manifested to us-what we have seen and heard we proclaim to you also, so that you too may have fellowship with us, and indeed our fellowship is with the Father and with His Son Jesus Christ (1 John 1:1-3).

Why are we afraid of relational discipleship? Could it be that we don't want to be exposed to our fears, shortcomings, failures, or perhaps weaknesses? Jesus actually slept among them, walked with them, ate with them, and trained them. The cross, death, and even His resurrection didn't stop the relational training that Jesus had with His disciples.

In the Old Testament, we see that Moses was willing to pour out everything into the life of Joshua. Joshua was able to see the "good, the bad, and the ugly" of Moses. Elijah asked Elisha to journey with him as a way to experience relational discipleship. In fact, the only reason Elijah let go of Elisha was because he was taken to heaven (2 Kings 2:11).

I often wonder if the effects of post-modernity and post-*Chris-tendom* (Christendom being a time when the Christian church occupied a central and influential role in society, and the Western world considered itself to be officially Christian) are contributing factors as to why we don't seek relational discipleship. Some of the approaches taken by post-*Christendom* leaders are actually reflections of secular programs, shows, and leadership attitudes, all of which fall short of the example left by Jesus. Are we rejecting our next generation? Do we think that we are too good for them? Do we see the potential in them in the same way someone once saw it in us? Some Hispanic ministers and lay leaders have taken the arrogant attitude of Hollywood celebrities. They are unapproachable, untouchable, and maybe un-trainable. They measure success by observing Sunday morning attendance instead of assessing how many true disciples they have trained.

There is a reality that I have yet to understand: if we as Hispanics are so relational, why are we afraid of relational discipleship? Some leaders invite people into their circle only by status and not by their potential. I do understand that things have changed and that we must protect ourselves from potentially vicious people who may threaten our lives inside the church. However, I ask this question: why we disappear after preaching a sermon titled "The need for discipleship," without even shaking hands with our potential apprentices?

Relational discipleship has benefits. It helps us to have a systematic discipleship training that allows the apprentice to personally relate with his mentor; to ask questions and seek advice; to see our mentor as a human, not a celebrity. The pioneers of our Hispanic denominations understood the importance of relational discipleship. The former founder of The Hispanic Assembly of God, H. C. Ball, trained Bazán, who later trained Girón, who subsequently trained Miranda, and the list goes on. What we are pursuing is a discipleship that develops not only knowledge, but also friendship. Jesus Christ was so attached to His disciples that He didn't just call them His disciples but His friends: "You are My friends if you do what I command you" (John 15:14). It is through friendship that we are able to identify with our people as Jesus did with His disciples. In his book, *Liderazgo y Amistad* (Leadership and Friendship), Jesse Miranda states, "The identification of the leader with the people is friendship."[11] Relational discipleship will also allow us to not only pass on our Hispanic heritage, our struggles, and our strengths, but also our exploits. Our E.H.G. is waiting, even crying out for leaders who will step into the spiritual ring and who are willing to pour out their knowledge, experience, time, resources, and life into them. After all, aren't they the future leaders of our Hispanic denomination?

Perpetual Relationship

Jesus's discipleship is the perfect example of a discipleship that is not only relational but also perpetual. From the moment He told them "Follow Me" until the moment He was ready to be taken to heaven, Jesus's relationship with His disciples was always a perpetual one. One of the last words uttered by Jesus is a testament to the everlasting love and concern He had for the disciples. He told them,

> If I go and prepare a place for you, I will come again and receive you to Myself, that where I am, *there* you may be also [emphasis in original]. Do not let your heart be troubled, nor let it be fearful. You heard that I said to you, "I go away, and I will come to you" (John 14:3, 27-28).

Jesus never stopped loving, caring for, and training His disciples. Although they abandoned Him on many occasions, Jesus always remained faithful and never gave up on them. The closing chapter of the Gospel of John expressed the perpetual love and relationship Jesus had with His disciples. He went to rescue them and to re-focus their calling: "Jesus said to Simon Peter, 'Simon, son of John, do you love Me more than these?' He said to Him, 'Yes, Lord; You know that I love You.' He said to him, 'Tend My lambs.' (John 21:15).

What I mean by perpetual relational discipleship is that it is a discipleship that we embrace with the understanding that our apprentices will learn from us at all times. Discipleship is not a part-time assignment, but a relatively full-time one. I am not talking about the fact that we may be working in our respective places of ministry on a part-time or full-time basis; however, we should view discipleship as a full-time commitment. A perpetual relationship is a perpetual commitment to those whom God has entrusted to us. Our E.H.G. may go through hardships, discontentment, and setbacks; however, it is our perpetual relationship that will never let them go and must stay with them at all costs. In the 1990s, I worked as an associate pastor of a church called Fuente de Vida (Fountain of Life). The senior pastor (Mizrahim Morales my brother) of that church was never afraid of pouring out his knowledge, friendship, and trust upon my life. What I learned under his ministry has encouraged me to pursue a relational discipleship style. Although we are both in different areas of ministry, we still communicate and when possible spend time together.

Another person that has been one of my mentors is Jesse Miranda. His mentorship began the moment he married my wife and I in 1985; he motivated me and helped me to enroll at Azusa Pacific University in order to obtain my master's degree in divinity. I remember on one occasion when I wanted it to quit, due to financial hardship, he said to me, "Maynor, I am not going to allow you to quit, if I have to pay for your tuition out of my pocket, I will. However, no matter what, you should finish your degree." In the year 2010, he officiated our 25th wedding anniversary, and in the year 2012, he attended the graduation ceremony for my Doctor of

Ministry degree. It has been a perpetual relationship and discipleship; I know I can call him at any time, with the confidence that he will always be there for me.

Relevant Discipleship

I remember the time when I used to play a video game called Pac-Man during my lunch hour. It was a thrill to chase Ms. Pac-Man around, and to be chased too. Several years have gone by and today, when I try to play or understand the latest games my young daughters are playing, they are nothing short of a challenge and a mystery to me. Some games even come along with a book or manual to show the players how to get the most out of the game. Another trend I am currently trying to comprehend is the language teens and young people are using when it comes to texting. For example, it was not until recently that I found out that keyboard characters and punctuations have different meanings in a typical texting conversation. For instance, the union between a colon and a close parenthesis, ":)", is an abbreviation for smiley face. If you want to add a nose to the smiley face, add a dash, ":-)". If you want to send a text hug, then it will look like this: (((H))). If you ever get a text that says 2G2BT, it means "too good to be true!"[12]

The point that I am trying to make is that games, technology, and the usage of language varies from generation to generation. When I was a teenager I never dreamed about the possibility of texting through a cell phone or doing my homework on a computer. I thank my children for forcing me to stay up-to-date with the new technology and trends among their generation. I tend to use the new technology for my own benefit, but most importantly, to stay relevant to the E.H.G. context when it comes to discipleship. Sadly, I will venture to say that a good number of leaders from previous generations do not make enough effort to stay up-to-date with all the issues concerning the next generation. By not staying connected with the younger generation, some leaders have the tendency to train their disciples through some methods and approaches that may not be relevant to the apprentices they are training.

Every time I read the Gospels, I'm so captivated with the relevancy by which Jesus spoke, taught, and communicated with His audience, and with His disciples. The language, alongside with real life examples used by Jesus, demonstrates that His style of discipleship was relevant to His epoch and to His disciples' cultural context. For example, in Matthew 4:18-19, Jesus saw two fishermen, Peter and Andrew, casting their nets into the sea. Since they were fishermen, Jesus told them "Follow Me, and I will make you *fishers of men* [emphasis added]." Do you think it was by accident that they left their nets and followed Him?

Why is it then, that we can't get our message across to the next generation? It is perhaps due to the fact that we understand neither their context and language nor their philosophy? The awareness of their generational context, in conjunction with learning how to speak their language, could prove beneficial to those engaged in E.H.G. training. What issues are affecting them, and what are their worries, ambitions, or goals? Often we forget that the world they are in is complex and mixed with opportunities as well as temptations. Their world is comprised of a promiscuous society, full of political confusion and financial challenges, to say the least. Adding pain to injury, they have to deal with issues pertaining to discrimination due to their minority status, and at times they find themselves at odds with both the Anglo and the Hispanic cultural societies.

The fact that we are Christians doesn't mean that we have to ignore these issues. Holland urges the church and its leadership not to overlook this problem, rather to understand what the role of the church and leadership should be. He states,

167

It is sometimes 'overlooked' by many Christians that churches are social institutions which reflect the beliefs, attitudes and behaviors of society at large, society itself being the incarnation of both good and evil in a matrix of individual and collective confusion and conflict. The ideal of what the Church ought to be is often confused with what it is in reality.[13]

Our understanding of the emerging generation's context will help us adjust our training strategies. One of our goals should be to help them develop a sturdy foundation made up of strong faith that will enable them to survive the future challenges and pressures of this world. David Kinnaman, Barna's Group president, wrote a note to today's leaders urging them to re-think their efforts with regard to properly training the next generation. He says,

As today's leaders, I believe we have an urgent responsibility to rethink our effort on behalf of the next generation of Christians. We hope young Christ followers develop a faith strong enough to last and to influence those around them. However, for too many, their faith does not survive in the real world. Simply put, we are not preparing today's teens and young adults for the kind of pressures they actually face.[14]

What are the areas that we need to look for in order to exercise discipleship with relevancy? I can think of at least three areas and those are social issues, civic spirituality, and religiosity.

Social Issues

The social context during Jesus's ministry was a hostile one; full of oppression against the poor, the needy, and the minorities. Everywhere Jesus went, He left a footprint of love, understanding, caring, healing, and hope. He fed the hungry (Matthew 14:13-21); He restored health to the sick (Matthew 9:1-13); He saved a woman condemned to death due to adultery (John 8:1-11); and He restored life to a widow's son (Luke 7:11-17). These are a sampling of the deeds He used in order to train His disciples.

As true Christians, we ought to recognize that true discipleship must include learning about and engaging in social issues. For too long we have accepted the idea that Christianity should only be limited to worship, exercising our spiritual gifts, or evangelism without community involvement. Although all of the above is correct, we forget that part of our discipleship training manual should include getting involved with our community, knowing the needs of our community, and doing something about those needs within our community.

Our relevant discipleship training should have the unchurched community in mind, for that is the context our new generation is currently facing. Robert Schuller, the former pastor of Crystal Cathedral, gives sound advice when it comes to relevancy and community. He states: "The unchurched people's need will determine our programs; the unchurched people's hang-ups will determine our strategy; the unchurched people's culture will determine our style; the unchurched population will determine our growth goals."[15] If I were to add one more sentence to Schuller's quote, it would be: The relevancy of the next generation will determine our discipleship approaches.

We need to ask ourselves the following questions: Do we know the needs of our community? Are we aware of its pain, sorrow, loneliness, or perhaps abandonment? When was the last time we had a conversation in order to find out how to engage in and with our community? It is easy to send people back to their communities with the gospel in their heart, but without doing anything about their social condition. Willard, in his book, *The Divine Conspiracy Continued*, in reference to social realities, writes,

> The local church must be moved from simply advocating understanding of or professing belief in the availability of life in the kingdom to demonstrating and manifesting a broader expression of what the gospel can accomplish when brought directly to bear on the weighty matters of our social realities. These matters are crucial and eternal, for they deal with the eternal souls of those individuals within our families, our neighbors, our society, and finally the world at large.[16]

Jesus came to establish God's kingdom on earth, and His kingdom was one of love, forgiveness, healing, and providing for those in need. Jesus ministered to the multitudes spiritually, emotionally, and physically, He fed the multitudes before sending them home (Matt. 14:21); He was moved to compassion when He saw a widow crying on her way to the cemetery to bury her only son. The Bible says that Jesus's heart "went out to her and said, "Don't cry" (Luke 7:13 NIV). Jesus raised him and gave him back to his mother.

One of the groups within our social context that is in need of our understanding and involvement is the undocumented people. I believe that they are part of God's kingdom. They are in need of our helping hand. We must reach out to them, for they also have social needs. Their hearts are broken and in need of not only hearing the gospel, but more so in need of our love and compassion. In my personal opinion, a social issue is one area that must be included when it comes to discipleship training for our emerging generation. In the same way that Jesus encountered an oppressed society, the Hispanic church has also experienced ethnic minority oppression. Therefore, as leaders, it is not beneficial to your apprentices to ignore this reality. The Hispanic leadership should play a vital role in this endeavor.

It is the church that can best understand and respond to these problems. Edwin Villafañe, in his book, *The Liberating Spirit*, understood this problem. He describes the role of the Hispanic church as an "oppressed ethnic minority." He says it is one that lives and works under a dominant church and society. Yet, it is a model for society in the following significant roles: (1) Survival, (2) Signpost, (3) Salvation, (4) Shalom, (5) Secrets of the Reign (6) Seedbed, and (7) Social Service Provider.[17]

Civic Spirituality

One of Jesus's quotes that is often used in relation to civic duties and to finances is, "Then render to Caesar the things that are Caesar's and to God the things that are God's" (Matthew 22:21). Jesus understood the Roman's dominion over Israel, and although He respected government authorities, He remained faithful to His father. Theologians have given many interpretations as to what Jesus tried to say. Some say that Jesus meant, "My kingdom comes first, then Caesar's," while others say that He wanted to teach about giving to God what belongs to God, and to Caesar what belongs to Caesar. One thing I know, Jesus was aware of His civic duties while on earth. He wanted to teach His disciples to obey earthly authorities. Paul, in His letter to the church in Rome, admonished us to obey the authorities established by God (Romans 13:1-7).

What is the role of a leader when it comes to civic duties, politics, and government involvement? Who does it depend on? I can personally tell you that in my discipleship training, I am well aware that we need to train the next generation to face many civic and political issues. I believe in civic participation as long as we show a Christ-like attitude. I desire that my disciples get involved, vote, and seek public offices.

During George W. Bush's presidential tenure (2001-2009), our U. S. Attorney General was John Ashcraft, a minister of the Assemblies of God. He served with dignity and wisdom when the United States was undergoing serious crises in the aftermath of the September 11 terrorist attacks. As Hispanic leaders, we need to train our young people to aim high spiritually, as well as prepare them to be leaders, not only in a church context, but also outside the church. As a pastor and a leader, I always call the children the "future evangelists, missionaries, and pastors," but also the "future lawyers, doctors, senators, or even presidents." If we expect to have 119 million Hispanics by the year 2060, let's prepare the next generation that will occupy a place in history in the near future.

Religiosity

Most of Jesus's debates and wrongful accusations didn't come from outside entities but rather from the inside ones. The Pharisees and Sadducees were among His fiercest enemies. A great portion of the Gospel is dedicated to Jesus's replies and encounters with them. At the end, they called for His crucifixion. Jesus took advantage of every single encounter with these people and showed His disciples how to deal with them. We find another significant example of religiosity in the book of Acts. During the Apostle Paul's missionary journeys, his enemies did not come from the outside, but from within. On one occasion, his religious enemies even enticed people to kill him (Acts 14:19).

I wish I could say that those issues are far behind us; however, that is not the case, for these issues are still very much alive among Christians. There have been churches that were divided because of minor religious conflicts within their congregations or within their respective denominations. Since the beginning of our Hispanic denominations, we have had and sadly will continue to have divisions, misunderstandings, fights, theological differences, legalism, and even discrimination. The next generations of leaders need to be trained on how to deal with these matters, because they are indeed real, and can damage God's kingdom. The leader opting not to train disciples on how to cope with these concerns is depriving them from learning valuable lessons that could prove beneficial to their training. The apprentice builds character and maturity through overcoming these negative circumstances, and learns how to develop endurance in their places of assignment.

First and second generations of Hispanic leaders within our denominations need to be an example to the next generation. Unity, love and mutual cooperation is what the Lord has called us to impart. We have a duty to not discriminate anybody based on sexual, ethnic, or social background, for we are all members of Christ's body. The Lord's intercessory prayer for His disciples was "that they may all be one; even as You, Father, are in Me and I in You, that they also may be in Us, so that the world may believe that You sent Me" (John 17:21).

In summary, let us not be afraid of the new methods, techniques or settings that are relevant to the E.H.G. When training the younger generation, I use every single aid I can find and try to relate my training to their context. Starbucks is not my favorite place to study, but if needed, I don't mind talking to my apprentices there while enjoying a cup of white hot chocolate.

Experiential Discipleship

The Gospel of Luke (10:1-22) explains that the Lord sent His disciples on an experiential journey. Seventy of His disciples received instruction and empowerment. After a last minute warning as to what to do and what not to do during their journey, they were released to go and put into practice what they had learned. The disciples came back excited, rejoicing, and ready to go for another round. I can see them in their amazement as they reported to Jesus about all the miracles that took place. This is what they said: "The seventy returned with joy, saying, 'Lord, even the demons are subject to us in Your name'" (Luke 10:17). The gracious reply which came from the lips of their Master was:

> "I was watching Satan fall from heaven like light-
> ning. Behold, I have given you authority to tread on
> serpents and scorpions, and over all the power of the
> enemy, and nothing will injure you. Nevertheless
> do not rejoice in this, that the spirits are subject
> to you, but rejoice that your names are recorded
> in heaven." At that very time He (Jesus) rejoiced
> greatly in the Holy Spirit, and said, "I praise you,
> O Father, Lord of heaven and earth, that You have
> hidden these things from the wise and intelligent
> and have revealed them to infants. Yes, Father, for
> this way was well-pleasing in Your sight" (Luke
> 10:18-21).

Allow me to ask this question: When was the last time that you, as a Hispanic pastor or lay leader, sent your apprentices or disciples to the mission field? What tools, empowerment, or authority do you send with them? Have they come back with joy and saying "even the demons are subject to us in Your name?" What Jesus's disciples experienced was experiential discipleship in action. This type of discipleship approach goes through development stages in which experiential discipleship is implemented. I concur with Clinton's three development stages of leadership, and those are:

174

Osmosis: the leader learns implicit philosophy experientially.

Baby steps: the leader discovers explicit philosophy through experience and philosophy.

Maturity: the leader formulates, uses, and articulates his/her ministry philosophy.

He/she passes on to others the key ideas and retrospective reflection of what ministry is about.[18]

Discipleship training is not complete until the apprentices undergo experience.

The meaning of the word experience, according to the Merriam-Webster's Collegiate Dictionary, comes from the Latin *experientia*, or, "act of trying." It refers to "knowledge obtained by doing; something that one has lived through"[19]. The Oxford Concise Dictionary defines experience as "an event or activity which leaves a lasting impression"[20].

All the training in the world, including training in theory and scholastic knowledge, or anything else, cannot compare to the everlasting impact of experiencing what has been taught. Can you imagine yourself receiving years of theory on how to drive, but never getting behind the wheel and not experiencing a nice drive? I can personally tell you of my first experiences in evangelistic crusades where I witnessed demon-possessed people set free, a young lady healed from her deaf left ear, a mute child who began to speak, people baptized with the Holy Spirit, and, most glorious of all, hundreds of people who received Christ as their savior. Nothing can compare to that experience!

Our next generation of leaders needs to see what the power of God is all about. If we call ourselves Pentecostals and are ministering under the gifts of the Holy Spirit, then let us lead them to the places and settings where they can also experience the same power and anointing. The Lord has blessed me with the privilege of visiting several countries, and many states within our own country. In my personal observation of some Hispanic churches, I have heard the outcry of the next generation. They are saying to us, "can you just let me preach, sing, teach, or pray for someone while you watch and observe?" Why are we so selfish at times? Why do we limit the potential of our youth? Why do we forget that we once were in the same predicament, and someone gave us an opportunity to experience what ministry is all about? When was the last time you gave your pulpit on a Sunday morning to one of your disciples or gave them the opportunity to teach a Sunday school lesson? The training cycle will never go around for the second time unless we are willing to allow our apprentices to have their own experience.

I agree with what James Garlow says in his book, *Partners in Ministry*, regarding training and experience: "If laypersons are to be involved in fruitful ministry, training is essential. Many times I have seen clergymen ask laypersons to fulfill important roles in the church without offering them any training opportunities-that is unfair."[21]

SUMMARY

The task of a leader is endless, yet fruitful. It demands consistency, effectiveness, a willingness to teach what is first taught, and the ability to stay on course no matter the cause. This and much more is expected of a good leader as a rabbi to others. Let me conclude this section by echoing Clinton's voice in regards to a good plan of action from an organized leader. He says:

Ask God to make you to be the kind of person who
will demonstrate these lessons in your own life...
Effective leaders maintain a learning posture.

Effective leaders value spiritual authority as a primary power base.
Effective leaders recognize leadership selection and development as a priority function.
Effective leaders who are productive over a lifetime have a dynamic ministry philosophy.
Effective leaders evince a growing awareness of their sense of destiny.
Effective leaders increasingly perceive their ministry in terms of a lifetime perspective.
Effective leaders are pace setters.[22]

Allow me to express my deep love for discipleship; for it is within my veins, my heart and my soul. I truly have faith in our next generation. They will accomplish great exploits for the Lord and have the potential to pave the way for one of the most glorious manifestations and harvests that mankind has ever seen before the Lord's return to earth. However, before they can go and experience God's power in their lives and ministry; our present leaders must first accept, embrace, properly mentor, train, and disciple them.

The best legacy we can leave our next generation of Hispanic leaders is one of discipleship. In keeping with the theme of approaches to leadership, we will move from discipleship to that of outreach. In the next chapter, I will explore the need for outreach among the different Hispanic generations and to the marginalized immigrants within the United States.

STUDY QUESTIONS

1. What is the Greek root of the word "disciple," and what is the definition of this word?
2. Name the four areas that comprise the discipleship quadrant approach.

3. If the choosing of Jesus's disciples was not by accident or coincidence, then how did He make His choices?
4. Name some of the benefits of relational discipleship.
5. Who provides the perfect example of a perpetual discipleship?

DISCUSSION QUESTION FOR GROUP STUDY

Consider the four areas of discipleship that comprise the quadrant approach. Share with your group the approaches that your church or denomination is using.

Chapter 10

Intergenerational Outreach

If we were to point out one area responsible for the Hispanic Church growth in the United States, it would definitely be **evangelism**. We are people who love and enjoy leading others to Christ. In fact, it has been, and will continue to be, the key to our growth. Both pastors and layleaders should commit to this endeavor. Evangelism among Hispanics is one of the factors for the continuing growth of our Hispanic denominations. Therefore, the recruiting of future leaders will depend in part upon our approaches and commitment to evangelism.

THE URGENT NEED FOR OUTREACH

As previously stated the projection of the future Hispanic population is enormous. By the year 2060 the Hispanic demographic will make up one-fourth of the total population in the United States. What this projection is telling us is that within the next forty four years; nearly one in every four people within the United States will be of Hispanic origin. I ask myself this question: **"In the future, are we going to have one Hispanic church for**

every four non-Hispanic ones?" This projection is a reminder of the enormous task that needs to be done. The Lord's command to His disciples, "Go into the entire world and preach the gospel to all creation" (Mark 16:15), is still relevant to Christians today. There may be different interpretations of this scripture; however, one thing is clear; millions of Hispanic and non-Hispanic people in the U.S. and around the world need to hear the gospel of Jesus Christ.

A few years ago, I was blessed to visit Rev. Wilfredo De Jesús's congregation, New Life Covenant (mentioned previously as the largest Assembly of God church in the United States). With its outreach to inner city Chicago, it serves as an excellent example of a church that has brought the gospel of Jesus Christ to a community in need. At the end of the service I had the opportunity to meet with him. I congratulated him for having the largest Assemblies of God congregation. Also known as Pastor "Choco," Rev. De Jesús provides a vivid testimony of what leadership development can do.

He began with a congregation of 120. At the present time, he is running an attendance of 17,000 people, with services in English and Spanish inside their brand new sanctuary. He loves to take his message to the brokenhearted people in his community in Chicago. His church has given birth to other churches; one of them is serving the African American community. The name of the church is New Life Covenant (daughter church), located in Chicago, founded in 2003. The name of the pastor is John F. Hannah, and the church is currently running multiple English services with thousands of attendees in each service. A few months ago, Pastor Hannah launched a new mission, offering bilingual (English and Spanish) services aimed at reaching the Hispanic community. My brother, Rev. Josue Morales, is the current pastor of this mission.

The Greek word used for gospel is *euaggelion*, meaning "good news"; the person preaching the gospel or the bearer of good news is called *euaggelistes*, "an evangelist, the one bringing good news."

The Lord has called the church to make disciples, but before they come, we ought to go and find them; bringing them to a place where they can start their walk with the Lord, that is one of the reasons why the church exists. Evangelism is one of the tools that can best accomplish this task. Gene Getz, in his book, *Sharpening the Focus of the Church*, says that the church exists to:

> ...carry out two functions-evangelism (to make disciples) and edification (to teach them). These two functions in turn answer two questions...When you ask, "Why does the church exist in the world?" you are asking what God expects to do through His people as they come in contact with the unbelieving world! When you ask, "Why does the church exist as a gathered community?", you are asking what God intends to happen to believers as they meet together as members of the body of Christ.[1]

In our evangelistic spectrum, there are at least three groups in need of an evangelistic outreach: The first generation of Hispanics, the **1.5**, the second generation, and the third generation, which is the emerging generation. Though they all come from the same ethnic background, each of the groups has unique characteristics. The first generation of non-Evangelical Hispanics usually only speaks Spanish. Their customs as well as their music preference and style are different from that of the 1.5 and subsequent generations. Most of the members of this group come from a Roman Catholic background. The next generational group is the 1.5 and the second generation. They have been able to assimilate the Latino and Anglo culture, most of them are bilingual, and they have no problem eating tacos or hamburgers.

Although their religious background continues to be Roman Catholic, they do not feel as attached to it as the first generation.

The third group is the emerging generation. This generation has fully embraced the Anglo customs and culture, often speak little or no Spanish; have different music styles, and if they go to a Catholic church, it is more of a tradition than practice.

The purpose of this overview with regard to the varying Hispanic generations is simply to bring forth the following point: we need an intergenerational and immigrational evangelistic outreach. The question the reader of this book may be asking is "Why intergenerational evangelistic outreach?" or, "What is intergenerational outreach?" I believe that the starting point of developing leaders is to aim to evangelize the world; a world that includes all of the Hispanic generations.

Intergenerational outreach is the reaching out to all the generations who are in need of the gospel of Jesus Christ. In the context of this book, I will say that intergenerational outreach is taking the gospel of Jesus Christ to all the Hispanic generations. As a leader, I fear that we may not be training our next generation of leaders to be intergenerational. The gospel must be preached to everyone and every race. I have observed that Anglo churches continue to reach out to all the Hispanic generations. It is not unusual to see Hispanic departments (missions or churches within an Anglo church) in Anglo churches where there is a Hispanic community, while we debate on planting new missions within our own communities.

A few years ago, a Hispanic denomination received an invitation from an Anglo one to open up new missions in a state where the community of Hispanics was growing rapidly, Alaska. They offered their churches and their resources to the Hispanic denomination; however, there was one condition: they required that all the missions be established under their administration and jurisdiction. As a pastor, I have personally witnessed the reality that once our 1.5 (generation), second, or emerging generation moves into an Anglo church setting, they have a hard time committing themselves to continue working within the Hispanic churches.

The Anglo churches have good structures, more resources, better facilities, and diversified ministries "which appeals to the higher acculturation level expectations of socially mobile Hispanic Americans."[2] Once again, I will reiterate that the gospel is meant to be shared for every culture on earth; however, I believe that the urgency of training the future leaders of our particular Hispanic denominations rest on our shoulders. It is our responsibility to do so. If we desire to have future Hispanic churches, it is imperative that we comply with God's calling to us to develop the next generation of Hispanic leaders.

It is not my intention to create animosity or separation between our Hispanic churches and our Anglo Churches; rather, my prayer is for an amicable comprehension that can lead to a healthy partnership that will harvest understanding and unity among each other. Clifton gives light, as well as a solution, to this dilemma in the following way:

> There is a serious need for Anglo churchmen to thoroughly evaluate the history of their relationship with Hispanic Protestant churches, to honestly recognize their numerous shortcomings, and to seek the revitalization of attitudes, strategies, and programs that will stimulate creative ministries and lead to mutually beneficial relationship between Anglos and Hispanic Americans and their respective churches.[3]

UNITY AMONG LEADERS

The unity among leaders representing all of the Hispanic generations is a matter that concerns me. If we aspire to accomplish the gigantic evangelistic task before us, it behooves us to recognize that we cannot achieve this commission alone. We definitely need each other, and should reach out to every Hispanic generation within our denominations.

The time to be self-centered, individualistic, and isolated has to come to an end. In my personal experience as a 1.5 generation leader, I see the distinct difference between the first, the 1.5 and second generation. Each generational group has its pride, and at times, its personal agenda. On one hand, the first generation claims to be of true Latino origin. On the other hand, the second generation claims to be American-born and proud to speak the local language, and the claims of both go on and on.

The problem that I see rests on the fact that if these generations do not reconcile each other's differences; eventually, everybody will be affected, including the E.H.G. I am concerned with the third generation, who is growing unattached to its Hispanic roots, and subsequent generations. The more unattached they become; the less interested they will be in Hispanic intergenerational evangelist outreach. Let us not lose focus on one of our missions as a Hispanic denomination, and that is to reach out to the lost through evangelism. John Stott, in his book, *Christian Mission in The World* said it this way,

> The cumulative emphasis seems clear. It is placed on preaching, witnessing and making disciples, and my deduction from this is that the mission for the church, according to the specification of the risen Lord, is exclusively a preaching, converting and teaching mission.[4]

What we are proposing here is a twofold solution: One is to have an outreach focus on the generational gap. We have, in our own Hispanic denominations, second generation ministers who are fully bilingual, bicultural, and bi-vocational. We also have a great number of first generation leaders and ministers who have experience and passion. Both of these groups can train the emerging generation on how to do effective intergenerational outreach. Let us remember that outside of the church are thousands of non-believers in need of salvation. The other proposal is an outreach which is aimed at the undocumented, including those who are and who will continue to arrive into the United States.

IMMIGRATIONAL OUTREACH

This group, the immigrants, is comprised of the first generation of Hispanics arriving into the United States, including the undocumented ones. Unconfirmed reports tell us that approximately 12 million undocumented people reside in the United States, and more will continue to arrive in the future. Amongst all people, our churches must reach out to this ever-growing group. The lack of intentional involvement towards this oppressed group brings sadness to my heart and spirit. Allow me to share this personal story:

In the capital city of Guatemala, Central America, in 2005, a band member confronted a Christian couple. The leader demanded that they pay around fifty thousand quetzales ($6, 600 local currency) within a few days. If they didn't' meet this demand, one of the family members would be killed. With great sacrifice and difficulty, the father was able to pay the demand. However, to his surprise, the gang came back with another demand for fifty five thousand quetzals ($7,300). The father tried to negotiate with the gang leader; he asked for them to reduce the amount, due to the fact that they did not have the cash. The gang leader's reply was, "You have ten days to come up with the money, and that is final!" The father didn't have the money. He was aware that the gang knew the whereabouts of every family member. He sold his little business (a Christian book store), and after being denied a visa to travel to the United States, he made one of the hardest, most dangerous decisions: to travel thousands of miles through the country of Mexico, with the hope of crossing the border as an undocumented alien. His main purpose was to save his family from death.

This scenario is one of many which cause Central and South American families to make the decision to travel to the United States of America; not to sell drugs or to engage in criminal acts, as many people would like us to believe, but rather to survive the enormous crises that our Latin American countries are facing. Sadly, many of these cases have the potential of ending in terrible tragedy.

John and his family, after crossing the border between Mexico and the United States led by a "coyote" (smuggler), found themselves in an unknown territory in the middle of the night, with no water or food. When his wife Maria began to dehydrate, the coyote ignored her plea for water; instead he said, "Keep on walking until we make it to the next town." Eventually Maria and her daughter Hanna found a little puddle; although the coyote told them that the water was for cows only, Maria and her daughter could not wait any longer. They had been walking for five days and the pain and thirst were more powerful than the danger of drinking contaminated water. The mother and daughter drank water from the paddle, unaware of the bacteria inside the contaminated water. A few hours later, Maria went into a state of shock, and eighteen hours after drinking the contaminated water, died in the middle of the night, in an unknown location.

John was faced with the heart-breaking dilemma of either staying alongside his wife's body or continuing his journey. With heavy pain, tears in his eyes, and with no shovels available, he and his two daughters, his son, and son in-law, buried their wife and mother with their bare hands, using only one empty can. It took them about five hours to open up a trench long and deep enough to put the love of his life and mother of his children in the ground. Afterwards, they kept on walking through the middle of the night, and this time alone, since the coyote disappeared, leaving them stranded in their journey, tired and exhausted. After taking a short nap, they were able to see a light up ahead, and walking toward the direction of the light, they found themselves around an oil well. They received food to eat and water to drink. As soon as they arrived, one of his two daughters collapsed with the same symptoms that caused his wife's death. An ambulance came, and his daughter was treated, and thank God, survived. However, they were turned over to the immigration authorities. With the help of a U. S. Customs officer, they went back to the place where his wife had recently died, and they unburied his wife's body.

John, his two daughters, son, and son in-law were granted a humanitarian temporary visa and allowed to bury Maria's remains for the second time; however, this time not in an unknown place but in a cemetery in the state of California. John and I have been friends since 1970, when we were still in Guatemala. When I heard the news, I attended the funeral. Just before the burial, John asked me something that I will never forget. He said, "Maynor, you are a pastor, so you can best answer this question. How is it that when running from death, I found it in the middle of the dessert?" I was speechless, and all I was able to say was, "John, I don't know the answer; however, the Bible says, 'And we know that God causes all things to work together for good to those who love God, to those who are called according to His purpose'" (Romans 8:28).

Later generations may not realize the struggles of their ancestors; therefore, it is our duty to share with them the story of our journey to the United States. It is also crucial to be aware of the fact that all Hispanic generations are in need of hearing the gospel of Jesus Christ. Evangelism is a vital component for effective outreach that eventually yields church growth. If we were to point out one area responsible for the Hispanic growth in the United States, it will definitely be evangelism.

I have shared this personal story to make the following point: Every day, hundreds of human beings cross the United States borders for various reasons and only God knows the exact reason why they do so. The media and even the government claim that we have at least twelve million undocumented people within the United States with hundreds crossing the border on a daily basis. It is my desire that Hispanics and Anglo denominations be more pro-active on behalf of our undocumented people. I have witnessed the lack of support and love amongst various conservative Christians towards them. Certain Christians have begun calling for their deportation and at times they have used the offensive derogatory slang word "wetbacks" (for the undocumented Hispanics, the word wetbacks is offensive). I pray that our next generation of Hispanic leaders will never forget that some of their ancestors were undoc-umented when they first arrived in the United States.

It is vital to remember that this group of people pioneered some of our churches. Such behavior and attitudes of these Christians mentioned above most certainly do not demonstrate God's love. We are aware of the fact that they have violated the law; nonethe-less, what are God's instructions to us concerning this matter? The Bible, in the book of Leviticus (19:33-34, NIV84), tells us how to treat the undocumented: "When an alien lives with you in your land, do not mistreat him. The alien living with you must be treated as one of your native-born. Love him as yourself, for you were aliens in Egypt. I am the Lord your God." I believe immigrants need to be embraced and never excluded. Our denominations and churches have a duty to continue reaching out to them.

The best way to treat Latino immigrants, whether legal or undocumented, is by opening our arms and embracing them as they are. Miroslav Volf in his book, *Exclusion & Embrace*, argues against exclusion by presenting some of the reasons why we exclude. He writes:

> We exclude also because we are uncomfortable
> with anything that blurs accepted boundaries,

disturbs our identities, and disarranges our symbolic cultural maps (Douglas 1996). Others strike us like objects that are "out of place," like "dirt" that needs to be removed in order to restore the sense of propriety to our world…We assimilate or eject strangers in order to ward off the perceived threat of chaotic waters rushing in.[5]

Embracing, Not Excluding

Allow me to give some reasons why we need to embrace the undocumented instead of excluding them.

We Must Do So Because They Are Victims of Political Unrest, Civil War, Abuse, Persecution, and Even Death

Economic factors play an important role as to why the undocumented feel they can no longer survive in their native country. One quick look at Mexico, Central and South American history regarding conquests that took place south of the U.S. borders, from the country of Mexico all the way to the southernmost South American country, will testify to the fact that Latino people have been the subject of many conquests.

Numerous conflicts have occurred in Latin American countries, resulting in a massive migration towards the U.S. Let's take the country of Guatemala as an example. Guatemala is one of five countries that constitute Central America. The local Civil War that took place in the middle of the 20th century paved the way for thousands of political refuges to head north, fearing for their lives. Thousands of refugees came to the United States as a result of the Guatemalan Civil War, which resulted in the death and disappearance of at least 75,000 people.[6] Political unrest sparked a civil war and a revolt in Guatemala, El Salvador and Nicaragua, that left thousands dead and many more heading to the United States. Juan Gonzalez writes that by the early 1980s, these countries were:

> ...all engulfed in wars... In El Salvador alone five hundred people a month were being massacred by the death squads. The carnage caused so many refugees to stream across the Mexican border...[7]

A great percentage of undocumented immigrants coming from Central American countries are not here to break the law or to traffic drugs, but rather are political refugees who only seek to survive. Leo R. Chavez in his case studies on cultural anthropology, called *Shadowed Lives: Undocumented Immigrants in American Society*, testifies to the fact that a great percentage of Central American undocumented immigrants are here for political reasons. He states, "A majority of the Salvadorans, Guatemalans, and Nicaraguans cited a reason for coming to the United States that included a reference to the political turmoil their country was experiencing..."[8]

Hispanic immigrants in the United States are now facing a dilemma that reminds them of the political disruption that they suffered in their own native countries. One of the biggest debates taking place in an unparalleled precedence is that of undocumented aliens. The biggest argument involves immigrants who have crossed the border without a proper visa. Those familiar with the guidelines and the requirements for acquiring a tourist, student, or working visa in order to come into the United States can testify to the fact that such visas are constantly and repeatedly denied by the U.S. consulate, especially to the poor, the needy, and even the victims of political persecution and threats.

Many undocumented immigrants embark on a journey towards the United States only after experiencing failure in their quest to acquire a visa. When their visa is denied, and when living in the face of political abuse, death threats, and fearing for their lives, the majority of them have no other choice but to cross the border as a way of survival. My friend whose wife died trying to cross the border had applied for a visa in Guatemala, but unfortunately their visa was denied.

The poor and afflicted among those wanting to immigrate have little chance of obtaining a U.S. visa. Fearful of the negative effects of illegal immigration, states most heavily impacted, like Arizona, have passed tougher immigration laws, such as its State Senate Bill 1070, directly affecting, discriminating, imprisoning, and deporting undocumented immigrants.[9]

At this moment, as we await the presidential election, undocumented immigrants are too easily subject to discrimination, labor abuse, and more so, are often used as political scapegoats. One political party appears to favor immigration reform, yet when they had the opportunity to pass the bill, they put it on the backburner. On the other hand, the other party uses immigration reform as one of the main issues for undocumented massive deportation. The real truth about undocumented immigration resides in the fact that not all the undocumented people crossing the border are criminals, drug lords, or fugitives of the law, but rather victims of political abuse, persecution, and, last but not least, **financial hardships**. Therefore, we as Christians ought to embrace them, and offer them a helping hand.

Hispanic Immigrants Should be Embraced, and Not Excluded, Because of Their Socio-Economic Status

Another factor forcing undocumented immigrants to take the risky and at times deadly journey towards the United States is the socio-economic factor. The socio-economic conditions, such as low wages, (it is not unusual to see a laborer get paid as little as three to four dollars per day), high infant mortality, shortened life span, and poverty, are great factors that force them to head north. Latino undocumented immigrants are facing their biggest challenges yet when it comes to their socio-economic status. Their levels of poverty, unemployment, and health conditions are rising rapidly. The conditions they face are no different than what the people of Israel endured during Jesus's times. Poverty, discrimination, hunger, and political abuse were prominent during Jesus's time on earth. Jesus always showed compassion, love, and protection toward the poor and the needy.

We Must Not Exclude Them, but Rather Love Them, Because They Are God's Little Children

There is a new wave of immigrants arriving to the U.S. This group has made the news in recent months; it is a group that is not comprised of adults but rather **unaccompanied children**. Last year I had the opportunity to visit one of the places where some of the Latino children are sheltered. Their stories testified to the fact that many children have taken the long and dangerous journey from their country to the U.S. either alone or with little sisters or brothers. It is heart-breaking. I was told that there was a nine-year-old girl that came with her eleven-year-old sister; and a 16-year-old mother that came with her infant baby, only six months old. I could not possibly fathom how or why parents can allow their children to take such a dangerous journey. These vulnerable children can easily become victims of crimes that may include sexual abuse. In 2014, an article by Pew Research reported the following regarding this situation:

> A record number of unaccompanied children have been apprehended along the U.S.-Mexico border since October, an influx so large that President Obama has called it an "urgent humanitarian

situation." To help house the overflow of children, emergency shelters have opened at military bases in California, Texas and Oklahoma, in addition to a facility in Arizona. And the U.S. Department of Justice on Friday unveiled a new $2 million legal aid program to help children navigate immigration courts. Between Oct. 1, 2013, and May 31 of this year, 47,017 unaccompanied children under 18 traveling without a parent or guardian were taken into custody, according to U.S. Customs and Border Protection. That total is nearly twice as high as all of the last fiscal year (24,493 apprehensions), with four months yet to go in the current fiscal year. One unofficial government estimate projects apprehensions rising to 90,000 in 2014—nearly four times as many as the year before.[10]

We can argue about the motives, or lack of rightful fear or judgment; however, we cannot argue the fact that they are already here, and in need of our love and our helping hand. This group of kids is in need of Jesus Christ. Their trauma and scars can only be mended by the power of love flowing from those who recognize that these little ones are also part of God's creation. They also need to hear the gospel of Jesus Christ.

Glen Stassen and David Gushee, in their book, *Kingdom Ethics*, testify to the fact that Jesus will always care for the poor and the needy. They say,

We see how God feels deep compassion for the poor and the outcast, when we see how Jesus was saying that God is working to deliver the poor from the misery and injustice that they experience. We see this in the way that Jesus and the disciples fed the poor, in the way the early church cared for the poor, and in the way some churches care for the poor now.[11]

Hispanic Undocumented Immigrants Should be Embraced, and not Excluded, Because They are God's Creation in Need of Love, Care, and Open Arms

The undocumented people living in the United States are often victims of discrimination, prejudice, and intolerance. Some people view them as intruders, criminals, drug dealers, and lacking proper education at the least. Consequently, these people argue that the undocumented are not worthy to remain in the land of the free, the United States of America. Although everyone is entitled to his or her own opinion and judgment, what breaks my heart is to see my Christian brothers and sisters stereotyping them, discriminating them, and no longer having tolerance for them. They find it easy to call for their deportation in order to solve the problem.

As we get ready for the 2016 presidential elections, my heart hurts when I hear some of the potential candidates, who claim to be born-again Christians, calling for the undocumented to be deported, and sent back to their countries, with no mercy or concern for either their well-being or the breakup of their families. I often wonder if these approaches are acceptable before the eyes of the Lord. My concern is not related to the breaking of the law since that is a given; my concern is with Christian leaders not seeing these people with love and compassion, as their brothers and sisters in the Lord or as potential believers for God's kingdom.

Perhaps the words of Willard's work *The Divine Conspiracy Continued*, in reference to love and compassion, are in order. He says, **"We must be able to value and love people as they are, whether or not we agree with their views or choices. Above all we are interested in their good and the goods that will**

194

contribute to their flourishing"[12] [bold added]. As Christians, we must all offer a helping hand to the undocumented. We must all be at the forefront of the fight against discrimination and prejudice. It should be a concern for local leaders including those who are Hispanics. We must show love and not hate, inclusion not exclusion. The church is called to demonstrate God's love and to teach the younger generation what true Christian leadership is all about. May the Lord help us to be a light in the darkness, and a helping hand to victims of discrimination.

As we come to the end of this section, let us realize that those of us professing to be true Christians quite frankly have no other choice than to embrace, love, and care for the Latino undocumented immigrants on the simple basis that they are God's creation. They are a people in dire need of being accepted and not excluded. What is it that makes us so out of touch with God's heart when it comes to arguments regarding laws and peoples' rights? Why is it that we fail to comprise the universal love of Christ for His creation in spite of race, skin color, or even legal status? Paul, in his arguments against discrimination and racial boundaries, admonishes us precisely against such non-Christ-like practices. Paul argues against such discrimination when writing to the Galatians, that we are all one in Christ, Jew or Greek, bond or free. When it comes to Christ, we are all one in Him, and that includes the undocumented ones. "There is neither Jew nor Greek, there is neither slave nor free man, there is neither male nor female; for you are all one in Christ Jesus" (Galatians 3:28).

It is essential that Hispanic leaders within the United States learn to embrace the Latino immigrants in their hearts, as Christ has accepted us as His. The ungodly approaches taken by some of our Christian brothers against undocumented and documented Latinos grieves my heart. Some Christians will dispute that Leviticus 19:33-34, when referring to the way we ought to treat the foreigners, does not include illegal aliens but only legal ones.

Jesus's approach towards the poor and needy was never discriminatory nor condemning, but rather loving and forgiving. The best way to treat Latino immigrants, whether legal or undocumented, is to open our arms and take them in as they are, and in so doing we share the good news of Jesus Christ.

THE HISPANIC POPULATION IS ONE OF THE BIGGEST MISSION FIELDS IN THE UNITED STATES

Jesus went through all the towns and villages, teaching in their synagogues, preaching the good news of the kingdom and healing every disease and sickness. When he saw the crowds, he had compassion for them, because they were harassed and helpless, like sheep without a shepherd. Then he said to his disciples, "The harvest is plentiful but the workers are few. Ask the Lord of the harvest, therefore, to send out workers into his harvest field" (Matthew 9:37-38, NIV).

Latino immigrants, especially the undocumented ones, usually arrive in the United States with no baggage, money, or even papers in their hands. Nevertheless, it is impossible for them to get rid of the baggage they hold inside their hearts. Crossing the border is a painful process in which they suffer emotional hurt and financial hardship. They leave their homes, families, friends, and relatives behind with only one goal in mind: survival. Leo Chavez in his book *Shadowed Lives* quoted G. Frank with the following words that best describe the risks of separation, anxiety, and dangers awaiting immigrants when attempting to cross the border:

When one family member leaves for the United States, family left behind experience some justifiable anxiety about the potential dangers of the journey. The worst case scenario is that the person is hurt or killed, with the family back home never receiving notification. This is not an idle fear. Undocumented border crossers often carry no identification so that if apprehended they can use a false name, avoiding a record of their arrest. But this also makes it difficult to identify the person in the event of an accident. Crossing the Border is filled with dangers. Bandits of both countries rob, rape, and even kill unsuspecting migrants crossing the border over the hills and through the canyons (Frank, 1979).[13]

A quick glimpse at the personal experiences, challenges, and suffering, (including discrimination, sexual and physical abuse undocumented immigrants are subjected to when crossing the border after arriving in the United States) gives us perhaps one of the best opportunities to engage in local mission ministry. This has the potential of becoming one of the greatest local mission ministries yet. Why? Let us explore some reasons.

Latino Immigrants Come to
the United States in Need of Healing

Understanding the needs of Latino immigrants is a vital tool that can lead to their healing. Documented or undocumented Latino immigrants come to the United States with a wounded heart in need of healing. If we consider them our enemies they will never be healed, and we may lose the opportunity to bring them to the knowledge of Jesus Christ. Even if we as Christians were to consider the undocumented Latino immigrants as our enemies, which they are not, we ought to engage in the ministry of mending their wounds, thus finding God in our enemies. Walter Wink, in his book, *Engaging the Powers*, challenges us to look beyond our enemies, and to find God in all people. He says, "I submit that the ultimate religious question today should no longer be the reformation's question, 'How can I find a gracious God?' But rather, 'How can we find God in our enemies.'"[14]

The pain that most of the immigrants are carrying inside is heart-breaking, and their emotional state at times is unbearable. Some of them come to us with shattered dreams, on top of wounded hearts. Women are often raped, and forced into prostitution as payment for crossing the border. By the time they arrive to the United States, their self-esteem is very low, and their hope of being successful has vanished. What they need is more than family therapy; they need **therapy for their souls.** McGoldrick and Hardy, in their book, *Re-Visioning Family Therapy*, narrated the painful experience of a Chilean woman leaving her seven-year old son behind:

> A Chilean woman, wearing a head scarf and quite emaciated, sits with her husband and their 2-year-old child in my office. This mother lost all of her hair very soon after leaving her 7-year-old son from a previous marriage in the care of her own mother in Chile. Since then, she says. 'I have been suffering from a *cancer of the soul* [italics added]." She has her son's framed photo face down in a drawer and cannot bear to make a phone call to him; her emotional suffering is so intense.[15]

Our Lord Jesus Christ came to heal the broken and the wounded. Jesus knew no borders, skin color, or race, and He never asked before performing a miracle, "Are you legal or illegal?" Christ went around healing everyone. In the same way, the Lord has called us to heal the broken–hearted. When Jesus came back from His forty days of fasting, ready to do ministry, He read a passage from the book of Isaiah, and unveiled what His mission on earth was all about. He said, "The Spirit of the Lord is upon me, because the Lord has anointed me to bring good news to the afflicted; He has sent me to bind up the brokenhearted..." (Isaiah 61:1). When the Spirit of the Lord is upon us, we will see undocumented Latino immigrants not as a threat in need of deportation, but rather as broken souls in need of healing through the anointment of the gospel of Jesus Christ. We must separate ourselves from selective evangelism, and move towards a relational one.

Latino Immigrants Come to the United States as Poor People in Need of a Helping Hand

When immigrants receive the devastating news that their visa petitions have been denied, not only is their world shattered, but more so, their financial state collapses. Some immigrants can pay up to $10,000 just to cross the border. They take on loans in their native countries at a high interest rate; such loans can take years to pay back. Immigrants will sell whatever they can in order to fund their journey towards the United States.

They are not only broken–hearted when they arrive, but more so, bankrupt, hungry, thirsty, lonely, and in desperate need of help. An article published by the Center for Latino Policy Research at the University of California, Berkeley, reports how much Guatemalan immigrants are willing to pay coyotes to cross the U.S. border:

The United States' tougher border enforcement policies since September 11 mean that most Guatemalans pay coyotes between $5,000 and $10,000 to get to the border, and an additional $1,500 to cross it. The journey is fraught with

199

danger, and most migrants are robbed by their own "guides" or suffer some kind of physical abuse by street gangs or security officials. The Guatemalan and Mexican media are also full of stories about migrants illegally transported in containers, who die from asphyxiation or dehydration.[16]

    A helping hand is needed because not all the immigrants have relatives in the United States, which creates a great need for ministry as they turn to the church for help. Ignoring their cry for help is ignoring Jesus Christ. Providing food, clothing, and shelter, to say the least, is perhaps a starting point for doing local ministry with undocumented Latino immigrants. We can't afford to miss out on the unique opportunity of presenting them with a practical and relational gospel. This gospel must not be limited to preaching only, but should include a gospel that follows with a humane and compassionate act of love towards all immigrants.

    Cesar Chavez was a son of immigrants from Mexico, who lived in Yuma, Arizona, during the 1930s. Chavez' parents had a farm, but lost it in 1938 and moved to California. They lived under a tent and in poor conditions, sometimes even inside their family car. Cesar grew up with a fighting spirit, and soon after seeing the conditions and abuses suffered by his people, the migrant workers called the brazeros, who had no health insurance, endured inhumane treatment, and earned low wages, he embarked on a journey with only one goal in mind: to organize farm workers into a nonviolent movement that would give them dignity and respect. This goal was accomplished when a union called United Farmers Workers Union (UFWU) was established.[17] If a labor activist was able to accomplish such task, we as Christians are called to do much more on behalf of the poor.

Jesus Christ on one occasion surprised His followers by stating that every time we help the poor and the needy, we are doing it as unto the Lord. He said,

For I was hungry, and you gave Me something to eat; I was thirsty and you gave Me something to drink; I was a stranger, and you invited Me in; naked, and you clothed Me; I was sick, and you visited Me; I was in prison, and you came to Me... Truly I say to you, to the extent that you did it to one of these brothers of Mine, even the least of them you did it to Me (Matthew 25:35-40).

Jesus Christ wants us to partner with Him in doing missions, in loving and caring for the poor. If we want to reach the undocumented immigrants for Christ, then we must work together in harmony as one body of believers and not as a politically divided entity. Undocumented Latino immigrants are in need of transformation. In fact, their hearts, souls, spirits, and even their financial state, are in need of transformation. This will begin to take place only when we are willing to embrace them instead of isolate them. Jesus commanded us to "love your neighbor as yourself." (Matthew 22:39) Brying L. Mayers, in his book, *Walking with the Poor*, clearly speaks about transformation through relationship, by loving and caring for the poor in this passage:

This is a commandment about relationships, not law; about who we must love, not simply what we must believe to do. This commandment must frame our approach to transformational development. It is both our motive for helping the poor

and point of departure from what a biblical understanding of transformation means; right and just
relationships.[18]

It is imperative to understand the basic truth regarding the
Gospel and the poor: the fact of the matter is that the poor are more
open to the Gospel, and the needy are more willing to give their
hearts to the Lord. If we want to experience revival as well as harvest for God's kingdom and if we want to do local missions, then
we must include undocumented Latino immigrants in our evangelistic vision. Most importantly, we must treat them as people in
need of help and friendship.

**Undocumented Latino Immigrants, Once They Receive
Christ, and are Discipled, Often Become the Best Witnesses
of the Lord Jesus Christ.**

They become bilingual, bicultural, and understand what hurt,
pain, loneliness and abuse is all about. They love to go to the
streets and share the Gospel to anybody in need of salvation. They
are responsible for the evangelical growth in the United States.
While some of the Anglos' evangelical denominations are losing
adherents, the Latino immigrant congregations keep growing in
an increasing manner.

I will conclude with a story of a mission field that has a glorious ending. I am referring to the opening of a new mission in a
church I pastored some years ago. One day, one of my deacons
came to my office with a heavy heart and with a huge burden over
his shoulder. He said to me, "Pastor, a few weeks ago I went to
the street called Elm, as I drove through the street, I noticed at
least 100 migrant workers waiting to be picked up by a contractor.
Pastor, the weather was against them, it was cold, chilly and some
of them didn't even have a jacket. Pastor, my heart has compassion

for these people. Can we do something about it?" My reply was, "What does your heart, alongside with the Holy Spirit, tell you to do?" His reply was, "to start a ministry that will give them bread, coffee, blankets, and a word of encouragement." I said, "Go ahead, you have my blessing and my support." It gives me pleasure to report that after three years of ministering to these people, as a result of this compassionate ministry, we signed a contract with an African American Church that opened their doors to us, and opened a new mission, that served the spiritual as well as social needs of all the migrant workers.

What are our priorities when it comes to undocumented Latino immigrants? What is the Holy Spirit telling us, or whispering in our ears during a time like this, when these immigrants are being persecuted and labeled not just as illegals, but more so as criminals? Once again, Schuller, the former pastor of Crystal Cathedral, gives sound advice when it comes to reaching out to our community, he states: "The unchurched people's need will determine our programs; the unchurched people's hang-ups will determine our strategy; the unchurched people culture will determine our style; the unchurched population will determine our growth goals."[19]

The choice is ours. I do not want the E.H.G. to forget this group, for they belong to their Hispanic heritage. If we fail to recall our roots, we may lose the richness of our Hispanic background. I hope and pray that the next generation of leaders will not overlook the first or the 1.5 generation, as well as the new wave of immigrants coming to the United States. Although there are fewer people crossing the borders every year, I believe that as long as there is poverty, war, persecution, and hunger in our Latin American countries, Latino immigrants will continue to arrive at the footsteps of our churches in need of a helping hand. Let us take hold of this great opportunity for evangelism, demonstrating God's love and compassion; in turn He will give us a great harvest for His kingdom.

On a personal note, I would like to express My utmost gratitude toward this country for truly being a land of opportunities. Most of the Christian community, as well as the secular ones, have been gracious to Latino immigrants regardless of their immigration status. Although I didn't come to this country as an undocumented immigrant; the United States has been a blessing to my life. I will always be grateful for God's calling on my life, and the leadership development that has taken place in this great nation called **The United States of America**.

STUDY QUESTIONS

1. Name the three groups in need of an evangelistic outreach.
2. Which Hispanic generation is comprised of immigrants, and according to unconfirmed reports, how many undocumented people reside in the United States?
3. What is the best way to treat Latino immigrants, whether legal or undocumented?
4. Name at least three reasons why the undocumented people need to be embraced and not excluded.
5. What are the reasons why undocumented Latino immigrants who receive Christ and are discipled often become the best witnesses of the Lord Jesus Christ?

DISCUSSION QUESTION FOR GROUP STUDY

Dallas Willard's work The Divine Conspiracy Continued, in reference to love and compassion, says, "We must be able to value and love people as they are, whether or not we agree with their views or choices. Above all we are interested in their good and the goods that will contribute to their flourishing." Use this quote to have a group discussion regarding the role of Christians towards the undocumented people in the United States.

CHAPTER PROJECT

Does your church or denomination have an outreach program to evangelize to the undocumented community? If they do not, assign a group of people to develop a strategy or program to evangelize to their undocumented community.

Chapter 11

Mentoring

I have been in ministry since 1979. From evangelistic crusades to youth conferences; and from pastoral ministry to teaching and preaching in different parts of the world; I can truly say that I am blessed with the opportunity to make a difference in other generations, especially in the area of mentorship, through discipleship. During the first phase of my ministry, it was difficult to find other ministers or leaders to mentor me; to give me an opportunity to develop and exercise God given ministerial gifts. It was hard to get bookings, let alone preach in major crusades. After giving many crusades locally and overseas, I found myself waiting for an opportunity to minister in a united crusade within my own denomination in the United States. It was during the first quarter of 1991 when that opportunity came.

Andrew, a pastor and leader of a section of churches in California, was in charge of organizing a united crusade. He had heard me preach before and graciously extended an invitation to me to be the main speaker for their united crusade. Most of the pastors participating in the crusade were not on board with him. Their argument was based on the point that I was too young, lacking experience and maturity to preach to their congregations and to their ministers; nevertheless, Andrew was persistent and finally convinced the pastors to give me an opportunity to be their crusade's speaker. He told them, "If the crusade is not successful, I will personally take the blame and the responsibility; however, I believe in Maynor, and I know that although he is young, the Lord will use him greatly; he will be a blessing to us all."

The crusade was a success. A great number of people accepted the Lord, church members as well as the pastors attending the event testified to the fact that they were ministered to. The church was so packed that a large number of attendees could not enter the sanctuary. They were led to the overflow area in order to hear the message. Others were not able to hear it from overflow, so they had to hear the service outside the church in the parking lot through a set of speakers.

I thank God for what He did in that crusade. I also appreciate Andrew who was willing to take a chance on me, he believed in me. As a result, not only was the crusade successful, but it paved the way for many invitations for other crusades. I will never forget Andrew. He was used by the Lord; the one that put his reputation on the line in order to give me an opportunity to minister at a higher level. We must view and treat members of our younger generation as leaders in the making; they are in need of mentors as well as leaders who are willing to take a chance on them. We must give them ministerial opportunities. Once they have received a proper training and mentoring, they need to be launched into deeper waters. They are like ships waiting to sail, never meant to stay anchored in the harbor. John A. Shedd once said, "A ship in harbor is safe — but that is not what ships are built for."[1]

As part of my research, I have had the opportunity to interview the three executive officers from an Assemblies of God Hispanic District. Each of them has articulated their burden for the E.H.G. In addition, they have also expressed three areas that are in need of our attention: "We need more young ministers in our district; we need more missions to be planted; and we need to mentor the next generation of leaders."[2] It is essential to note that we have been addressing these concerns through the course of this project's development. In the last section of this book, I would like to emphasize the need for two programs in our Hispanic denominations that could help transition this book from theory to practice.

The first program will focus specifically on mentoring the future leaders of the E.H.G. The second program will concentrate on the need to open a Hispanic Center for Leadership Development (H.C.L.D.). For example, Mission Ebenezer, under the leadership of Isaac Canales (as previously mentioned) is a true example of mentorship among the E.H.G. He has mentored two of his third generation sons, who are currently working as associate pastors alongside him, one of whom was offered a contract by a major league baseball team, but rejected it in order to answer the call to ministry.

MENTORING PROGRAM

What is mentoring? It is a process by which an older or mature leader identifies with another person, who is usually younger, and takes on the responsibility of pouring out his experiences, successes, or even failures in their lives. One of the goals of a mentor is leadership development. Clinton gives the following definition of mentoring:

> Mentoring refers to the process where a person with a serving, giving, encouraging attitude (the mentor) sees leadership potential in a still-to-be-developed person (the protégé), and is able to promote or otherwise significantly influence the protégé along to the realization of potential.[3]

In our previous segment, I introduced the concept of a quadrant model for discipleship (intentional, relational, revenant, and experiential). In essence, the proposed mentoring program will hopefully be a plan of action that will ensure implementation of the previously specified discipleship quadrant. I believe that every leader is given the mandate to identify future candidates for leadership within their respective ministerial communities. It is vital to note that we can noticeably see the mentoring strategies taking place throughout the Bible narratives. Significant examples of mentorship are when Moses mentored Joshua, Jesus mentored His disciples, and when Paul mentored Timothy. Currently, we have pastors and lay leaders in our Hispanic denominations whose valuable experiences in ministry can be beneficial towards promoting and exercising mentorship. You don't have to be an expert in order to influence and mentor someone else. In their book, *Connecting*, Paul Stanley and Robert Clinton invite leaders to engage in a mentoring process that will change and transform lives. They state,

> You don't need to know 'all the answers' or assume a teaching role to be a blessing to a mentee. Listening, affirming, suggesting, sharing experiences, and praying together are invaluable contributions that give a young mentee confidence, perspective, and practical help.[4]

Mentoring helps the future leader engage in personal leadership development alongside his mentee. The positions that our future generation will occupy require a training that is proper and personal. Sam Farina, an evangelist and a certified coach, says that young leaders often benefit from shadow coaching, where the coach observes the leader in her day-to-day activities and gives immediate feedback.[5] Why should we coach our younger generation? Sam asserts that, "Young people today are being thrust into leadership positions that require wisdom and maturity far beyond what one could expect from them, given their age and experience."[6] I am pleased to report that one Hispanic denomination, the Northern Pacific Latin Assemblies of God (NPLAD), has recently proposed a mentoring ministry aimed at the E.H.G. The name of this new ministry is Influence With Impact (IWI) and their motto is "Our Lives, His Call." Their mission and vision statements read as follows:

Mission Statement
IWI is committed to the forming of a Mentor's Ministry at every local church by focusing on identifying, developing and mentoring the emerging young leaders within the body of Christ; With the purpose of leading, building, and taking the church or ministry to the next level.

Vision Statement
IWI will help with the shaping of people who will shape our world.
IWI will help in the developmental process of mentoring.
IWI will help with the spiritual formation of mentorship.
IWI will commit to provide adequate resources to help both the mentor and mentee in this process.[7]

This mentoring program has been recently adapted by NPLAD district. We believe that this program has the potential of encouraging our next generation to begin their journey into ministry.

HISPANIC CENTER FOR LEADERSHIP DEVELOPMENT

All Scripture is inspired by God and profitable for teaching, for reproof, for correction, for training in righteousness...
(2 Timothy 3:16).

In the narrative of the Old Testament, we learn that the prophet Elijah had a center for leadership development, called "The school of the sons of prophets" (2 Kings 2:3-15). In the New Testament, a rabbi by the name of Jesus had a mobile school of ministry with at least twelve students. From the 1920s until today, at least four previous superintendents in our Latin American Assemblies of God have played an important role in the development of new leaders for the next generations. H.C. Ball was the founder of the Latin American Bible Institute (LABI) in 1926; Bazán relocated the two centers and placed one of them in Los Angeles; Jose Girón connected the LABI institution with the U.S. government in order for it to get more benefits; Jesse Miranda built the LABI dorms and established the Latin American Theological Seminary (LATS), as well as a Center for Hispanic Leadership. These efforts have yielded a great harvest of pastors, ministers, and leaders that are presently serving in different areas of ministry.

What educational legacy will the Hispanic leaders and their respective denominations leave to the next generation? We the Hispanics are labeled as a group that loves "on-the-job-training."[8] Although "on-the-job-training" is good, we still lack theological training. In general, we don't like to read, write, or sign up in a seminary in order to gain a theological formation. Nevertheless, I have faith in our next generation of leaders, for they will make a great difference in the future. I strongly believe that they will be the future Christian writers, professors, theologians, and apologists. They will make the Hispanic Christian population proud. In the meantime, it is our duty to pave the way for their theological formation.

A professor of one of my leadership classes at Azusa Pacific University asked us to write a paper concerning my future leadership goals (Fall 1997, Professor Gordon Coulter). I wrote about my desire to open a Hispanic educational center. What I didn't know at the time was that I would actually be opening a center for leadership development. I have been blessed with the opportunity to pave the way for the opening of a Hispanic Leadership Center, which has been instrumental in harvesting future leaders. In the past, institutions such as Vanguard University, Fuller Theological Seminary, Latin American Bible Institute, and Latin American Theological Seminary have joined efforts with New Dawn Worship Center (the church I pastored for over 15 years) to train future leaders.

This center targets the first generation of Hispanics on two different levels: the first is through a Bible institute called the Latin American Bible Institute (LABI San Jose) and the second is through a theological seminary called the Latin American Theological Seminary (LATS' Fremont extension). We have also teamed up with Fuller Theological Seminary, which is currently offering a Master's program in Spanish (this institution has recently moved to a new location). Although I'm grateful for all of these accomplishments, there is one important component missing: a Hispanic center that aims to equip the next generation of leaders. Unfortunately, we must admit that we don't have enough or any Hispanic institutions in our denominations that are responding to this specific task.

We are grateful for LABI, LATS, Azusa Pacific University, Vanguard University, Northwest University, Fuller Theological Seminary, and other Theological Seminaries and Christian Universities, which have paved the way for ministerial training; however, we are in need of an institution with a primary goal of training the emerging generation of our growing Hispanic denominations. In the same way that the previous institutions have been established to serve their generations, our leaders should make an effort to establish an institution for the subsequent generations.

Since I'm a dreamer, I envision a future Christian Hispanic University, a Hispanic English denomination, and a Hispanic center that serves the emerging generation. Our present Hispanic Christian institutions for the most part are only serving the first and the 1.5 generation. The classes are only in Spanish, and these institutions belong to other districts. Therefore, the opening of the center that I envision is vital and urgent. The Bible says "Iron sharpens iron, so one man sharpens another" (Proverbs 27:17), and in the same way, the Hispanic center can focus its efforts on sharpening and equipping the next generation of leaders.

Some of our youth are currently exiting our churches in search of a relevant theological training. Their quest for ministerial training takes them to some institutions that are not sensitive to the Hispanic challenges; furthermore, their Biblical or theological training does not always have a Hispanic vision in mind. I thank God that the schools of theology where I have received my theology education have always challenged me to go back and serve my Hispanic Christian community. In the following pages I will present a short model of what a Hispanic center will be comprised of.

This Center Will Aim to Enlist Students Who are High School Seniors

One critical statistic states that at least 70 percent of senior graduates who have enrolled in colleges will depart from their faith.[9] We can argue about whether this statistic is accurate or not, however, one thing is clear, and that is the need of a center that seeks to change these statistics by inviting high school seniors to give at least one year of their future life unto the Lord. After their senior graduation, they will be asked to commit to at least one year full time training at the H.C.L.D (Hispanic Center for Leadership Development).

Some years ago, I read the above statistic. It not only shocked me but more so broke my heart. Sixty to seventy percent of high school students transitioning from church to college never come back to church. Although this statistic may or may not be accurate, I took it seriously. I did some research and purchased a book called *How to Stay Christian in College*, and I opened a weekly Bible study at my home. Out of all the high school and college students that attended this Bible study, I am happy to report that all of them are serving the Lord. The majority of them are church leaders and faithful members. Although some of them for work related reasons or moving to other locations are no longer in the mother church, they are active in their respective churches. We have students that have or are currently enrolled in prestigious Universities such as: Berkeley, Harvard, and Columbia to say the least.

A Biblical Curriculum That is Relevant to the Emerging Generation

The curriculum will consist of at least 18 units of Bible courses, 12 units of theology, 15 units of church ministry courses, and 16 units of leadership courses. Upon completion of these units, the student will get a diploma in Biblical leadership studies.

General Education Curriculum

The goal of this curriculum is to provide the students with general education courses that are transferable to junior colleges or four-year universities. If the students wish to pursue different majors, they will at least have a good head start. Oftentimes

Christian universities are willing to give credit to students who have taken Biblical courses.

Off-Campus Online Classes and Polycom

This program can be an option for students who, for any reason, are not able to attend the Hispanic center, but are still willing to enroll in the leadership program. Aside from the fact that students will be able to sign up for the online classes, they will additionally be able to have the option to take their classes with the assistance of communication technology like Polycom. Polycom is a technological system that allows students anywhere in the world to participate in classes in which they can interact. The goal of this system is to enhance the spectrum of how classes are offered as well as to take advantage of the latest technology available.

Classes Will Be Offered in English

Our current institutions offer their classes only in the Spanish language. Therefore, this program has been developed with the E.H.G. in mind. What we are currently proposing is a program that is offered in English.

A Branch for First Generation Students

We have first generation ministers, leaders, and laypeople in need of training. Most of this group does not have the time or the resources to attend an on campus institution. I believe that the system that works best for them is through extensions. That way, students will be able to take off-campus classes in Spanish.

Accreditation

The H.C.L.D. will initiate the long-awaited process of achieving an accredited Hispanic institution. Azusa Pacific University, where I commenced my studies in 1992, was formed in 1930, under the name of Los Angeles Pacific College. Today, it is a fully accredited institution and serves thousands of students in different locations. Thanks to the leadership and efforts of Enrique Zone, Associate Dean for Regional Centers and Multicultural Programs at Azusa Pacific University, at the present time Hispanics attending the university can now enjoy their brand new center for theological studies. This center is dedicated to training pastors and leaders from different denominations.

Additionally, the H.C.L.D. will seek a partnership with an accredited institution for two reasons: first, to give students accredited and transferable general courses, and second, to forge agreements with Christian colleges or universities to give the students credits toward pursuing a higher degree in theology or ministry.

Scholarship Funds and Government Loans

Our Hispanic denominations will promote a scholarship fund where churches, ministries, and individuals can donate money towards this cause. Partnering with an accredited institution would allow our students to get government loans; thus, they will be able to pay for their tuition.

A Building for the Hispanic Center

The growth of our Hispanic denominations requires the purchase of a new building or the construction of new offices. It is my hope that leaders and members of our vast Hispanic denominations consider searching for new property with the hope of accommodating not only our future Hispanic Center for Leadership Development, but also other centers with the help of their respective denominations.

SUMMARY

I would like to make the following reflection: what I've presented is merely a preliminary sketch of what could hopefully become a Hispanic center. It's a model that could use adjustments and improvements. The format of mentorship presented is perhaps the beginning of what could possibly become one of the first Hispanic institutions that emphasizes leadership for the E.H.G.

I believe that our Hispanic denominations should have a school of leadership. It doesn't have to be a big school with a grandiose facility at the beginning. Our churches should partner with their respective denominations in order to achieve this goal. As Eddie Gibbs, in his book, *Church Next*, comments, "The task of the seminary is to work alongside with churches to assist in resourcing them for their manifold ministries in diverse missionary situations in a rapidly changing world."[10] It is important for every church or ministry leader to have at least a program or system where systematic Bible training takes place. The H.C.L.D is the answer to this need.

In December of 1900 a group of students who attended a Bible school at Topeka, Kansas, underwent a study about the day of Pentecost in Jerusalem.[11] This study culminated with the outpouring of the Holy Spirit upon their lives and was possibly the birth of Pentecostalism in the United States. May our emerging generation, through a systematic study of God's word, usher an unprecedented visitation of God upon their lives, and upon the world.

STUDY QUESTIONS

1. What is mentoring?
2. What is the mission statement of the proposed Northern Pacific Latin Assemblies of God mentoring program aimed at the emerging Hispanic Generation?
3. According to a critical statistic, what is the percentage of high school graduates who have enrolled in college that will depart from their faith?
4. What is a Polycom system?
5. What are some of the questions that remain unanswered and in need of more research as described in the conclusion section of this book?

DISCUSSION QUESTION FOR GROUP STUDY

Does your church or your denomination have a center or training program aimed towards the emerging generation? Share the program with your group. Otherwise, discuss the possibility of creating one.

Conclusion

H ispanic denominations have been blessed with leadership development strategies that have proved to be effective and fruitful. However, the necessity to embrace new approaches with the E.H.G. in mind is inevitable. We can no longer ignore the need to train the next generation of leaders. The goal of this book is to create an awareness of the need for new leadership development approaches in the following areas: spiritual formation, discipleship, intergenerational, and immigrational leadership outreach, mentoring ministry, and theological education. During the process of writing this book, I came to the conclusion that I have barely scratched the surface of the problem. There are still many questions that remain unanswered and the need of more research is in order. Some of the questions for future research and consideration are:

> What will be the **generational makeup** of our Hispanic leadership denominations in the year 2060? What languages will be spoken? What would be our relationship with the Anglo churches and their leadership?

Are we going to pave the way for an **English Hispanic Denominations?** And in light of these questions; what new approaches are in need of consideration?

A few years ago, my wife and I had the privilege of visiting the University of Oxford in England. My desire was to visit the place where John Wesley, the founder of the Methodist movement, received his education. To our surprise, our tour took us to a place called "The Wesley Room," perhaps the place where he had spent countless hours studying. After my visit, I came out of that room with a sense of gratitude and a lesson of his legacy. My first thought was, "If Wesley only knew the legacy he left behind." H.C. Ball, the man responsible for the birth of the Latin American Assemblies of God, received God's calling to Hispanic ministry in a Methodist church when he was only fourteen years of age. I believe that if the E.H.G. is properly trained, it has the potential to follow Wesley and Ball's legacy. In the same way, Hispanic denominations owe an endless gratitude to our pioneer leaders whose courage, integrity, and hard work have paved the way for the formation of our Hispanic denominations. I pray for their leadership legacy and the fruit of their hard labor never to end; to continue soaring unto the next generation.

The future of our Hispanic denominations will depend on the decisions made today. We have in front of us a great task and a unique opportunity to make a difference in the U.S. and in the world. If the Lord's return does not take place before the year 2060, we will see a tremendous increase of Hispanic population in this country. We will have as much as 119 million Hispanic people living in the U.S. Our E.H.G. will be different than the Latino generation that came to the United States many years ago.

The emerging generation will include elite professionals, politicians, Christian pastors, teachers, theologians, scholars, and perhaps apologists. The future Jonathan Edwards, John Wesley, Billy Graham, H. C. Ball, and [insert the name of a great leader of your denomination] has been born already; they only need to be mentored, discipled, and sent. It behooves us to pay attention to what is taking place right now; to take leadership development seriously; to invest time, resources, and prayer on behalf of this generation. We have the choice of winning them, training them, and making them our disciples, or else the world and the secular academic institutions will change their young minds and hearts, resulting in dreadfully lost generations.

Therefore, let us equip the next generation of leaders, and I believe that they will yield the greatest harvest of souls and churches; one that is beyond our imagination. New frontiers must be reached; more souls need to hear the gospel of Jesus Christ; more discipleship needs to be done; and more new missions need to be planted. Let us never be afraid of pouring out our lives, experiences, and resources toward our next generation. Moses left his leadership legacy with Joshua; Elijah with Elisha; Jesus with His twelve disciples; and Paul with Timothy and others. **Who are your followers? Who is your mentee? Who will carry your legacy?** I feel an utmost responsibility to the E.H.G., of which my two daughters are a part. It is my prayer for this book to contribute to anyone willing to engage in leadership development for the future generations. It is with great humbleness and with a sense of urgency that I present this book for your review and for your consideration.

Habakkuk 3:2 says:

"Lord I have heard the report about You and I fear;
Oh Lord revive Your work in the midst of the years,
In the midst of the years make it known…"

Notes

INTRODUCTION

1. Virgilio Z. Arceyuz, *Historia De La Iglesia Evangélica En Guatemala* (Guatemala, C.A.: Genesis Publicidad s.a., 1982), 133.
2. Ibid.
3. Sharon R. Ennis, Merary's Rios-Vargas and Nora G. Albert, "The Hispanic Population: 2010," U.S. Census Bureau (May 2011): 2, http://www.census.gov/prod/cen2010/briefs/c2010br-04.pdf (accessed February 1, 2012).
4. Jens Manuel Krogstad, "With fewer new arrivals, Census lowers Hispanic population projections," *Journal of Pew Hispanic Center* (December 16, 2014): 1, http://www.pewresearch.org/fact-tank/2014/12/16/with-fewer-new-arrivals-census-lowers-hispanic-population-projections-2/ (accessed April 18, 2016).
5. D'Vera Cohn, "Future immigration will change the face of America by 2065," *Journal of Pew Hispanic Center* (October 5, 2015): 1, http://www.pewresearch.org/fact-tank/2015/10/05/future-immigration-will-change-the-face-of-america-by-2065/ (accessed April 20, 2016).
6. Elizabeth Huff, "In matters of style, swim with the current...(quotation)," *Thomas Jefferson's Monticello* (June 8, 2011): 1, https://www.monticello.org/site/jefferson/matters-style-swim-currentquotation (accessed April 20, 2016).

Chapter 1

1. The World Book Encyclopedia, s.v. "Juan de Oñate" by Richard A. Bartlett. Harvard Encyclopedia, s.v. "Spanish," p. 953., quoted from Daniel Sanchez, *Hispanic Realities Impacting America: Implications for Evangelism & Missions (*Fort Worth, Texas: Church Staring Network, 2006), 66.
2. Wikipedia, "Treaty of Guadalupe Hidalgo," http://en.wikipedia.org/wiki/Treaty of_Guadalupe_Hidalgo (accessed February 21, 2012).
3. Sanchez, *Hispanic Realities Impacting America,* 4-5.
4. Sharon R. Ennis, Merary's Rios-Vargas and Nora G. Albert, "The Hispanic Population: 2010," *U.S.Census Bureau* (May 2011): 3, http://www.census.gov/prod/cen2010/briefs/c2010br-04.pdf (accessed February 1, 2012).
5. Cohn, "Future immigration will change," 1. Krogstad, "With fewer new arrivals," 1.
6. Cohn, "Future immigration will change," 1.
7. Krogstad, "With fewer new arrivals," 1.
8. Cohn, "Future immigration will change," 1. Krogstad, "With fewer new arrivals," 1.
9. Ibid., 4.
10. Jens Manuel Krogstad and Mark Hugo Lopez, "Hispanic population reaches record 55 million, but growth has cooled," *Journal of Pew Hispanic Center* (June 25, 2015): 1, http://www.pewresearch.org/fact-tank/2015/06/25/u-s-hispanic-population-growth-surge-cools/ (accessed April 18, 2016).
11. Ennis, Vargas, "The Hispanic Population: 2010," 3.
12. U.S. Census Bureau, "The Hispanic Population in the United States: 2010 Detailed Tables," Table 1, http://www.census.gov/population/www/socdemo/hispanic/cps2010.html (accessed February 23, 2012).
13. U.S. Census Bureau, "American Community Survey 2010," B01002H, http://factfinder2.census.gov/faces/tableservices/jsf/pages/productview.xhtml?pid=ACS_10_1YR_B01002H&prodType=table (accessed February 23, 2012).
14. Jie Zong and Jeanne Batalova, "Frequently Requested Statistics on Immigrants and Immigration in the United States," *Migration Public Institute* (April 4, 2016): 5, http://www.migrationpolicy.org/article/

frequently-requested-statistics-immigrants-and-immigration-united-states (accessed April 25, 2016).

15. Nicholas Jones, "U. S. Census Bureau News Report," (March 24, 2011): 22, http://www.census.gov/population/www/socdemo/hispanic/cps2010.html (accessed February 23, 2012).

16. National Vital Statistics Reports, Vol. 64, No. 1,"Births and birth rates, by Hispanic origin of mother and by race for mothers of non-Hispanic origin, United States 1989-2013," Table 5, http://www.cdc.gov/nchs/data/nvsr/nvsr64/nvsr64_01.pdf (accessed April 22, 2016).

17. U.S. Census Bureau, "The Hispanic Population in the United States," Table 8.

18. National Vital Statistics Reports, Vol. 64, No. 1,"Births and birth rates of unmarried women, by age and race and Hispanic origin of mother: United States, 1989-2013," Table 15, http://www.cdc.gov/nchs/data/nvsr/nvsr64/nvsr64_01.pdf (accessed April 22, 2016).

19. Pew Research Center tabulations of 2014 American Community Survey, "Statistical Portrait of Hispanics in the United States, 2014," Table 1, http://www.pewhispanic.org/files/2016/04/Statistical-Portrait-of-Hispanics-in-the-United-States-2014-final.pdf (accessed April 22, 2016).

20. Ibid. "Homeownership and Household Characteristics," Table 32.

21. Ibid. "Educational Attainment and Enrollment," Table 17.

22. Ibid. "Educational Attainment and Enrollment," Table 20.

23. Mark Hugo Lopez, "Latinos and Education: Explaining the Attainment Gap," *Journal of Pew Hispanic Center* (October 7, 2009):1, http://pewresearch.org/pubs/1368/latinos-education-explaining-the-attainment-gap (accessed February 27, 2012).

24. Richard Fry and Paul Taylor, "Hispanic High School Graduates Pass Whites in Rate of College Enrollment," *Journal of Pew Hispanic Center* (May 9, 2013). http://www.pewhispanic.org/2013/05/09/hispanic-high-school-graduates-pass-whites-in-rate-of-college-enrollment/ (accessed April 22, 2016).

25. National Gang Center. "National Youth Gang Survey Analysis," *Journal of National Gang Center*: 1. http://www.nationalgangcenter.gov/Survey-Analysis (accessed April 22, 2016).

26. U. S. Census Bureau, "Language Spoken at Home by Language: 2008," Table 53, http://www.census.gov/compendia/statab/2011/tables/11s0053.pdfIbid (accessed February 27, 2012).

Chapter 2

1. Sam Farina, "Coaching Next-Generation Leaders" *Journal of Enrichment* 17, no. 2 (Spring 20012): 78.
2. Clifton L. Holland, *The Religious Dimension In Hispanic Los Angeles: a Protestant Case Study* (South Pasadena: William Carey Library, 1974), 54.
3. Manuel Ortiz, *The Hispanic Challenge: Opportunities Confronting the Church* (Downers Grove: Intervarsity Press, 1993), 84.
4. Jeffrey S. Passel and D'Vera Cohn, "A Portrait of Unauthorized Immigrants in the United States," *Journal of Pew Hispanic Center* (April 14, 2009):1, http://pewhispanic.org/reports/report.php?ReportID=107 (accessed February 29, 2012).

Chapter 3

1. James Strong, *The Exhaustive Concordance of the Bible : Showing Every Word of the Test of the Common English Version of the Canonical Books, and Every Occurence of Each Word in Regular Order* (electronic ed. Ontario: Woodside Bible Fellowship., 1996).
2. R. L. Harris., G. L. Archer, & B. K. Waltke, eds., *Theological Wordbook of the Old Testament* (Moody Press: Chicago 1999), 844. CD-ROM (Logos Research System, Inc., 2002).
3. Ibid.
4. Ibid.
5. Ibid.
6. Concise Oxford Dictionary of Literary Terms, 2d ed., s.v. "Development."
7. Bobby Clinton, *Leadership Emergence Theory: a Self-Study Manual for Analyzing the Development of a Christian Leader* (Altadena, California: Barnabas Resources, 1989), 7.
8. Paul J. Kissling, *Reliable Characters in the Primary History: Profiles of Moses, Joshua, Elijah and Elisha* (England: Sheffield Academic Press, 1996), 44.
9. Matthew Henry, *Matthew Henry's Commentary on the Whole Bible: Complete and Unabridged in One Volume* (Peabody: Hendrickson, 1994), 506.
10. R. Jamieson, A. R. Fausset, D. Brown, & D.A. Brown, eds., *A Commentary, Critical and Explanatory, on the Old and New*

Testaments. On spine: Critical and Explanatory Commentary (Oak Harbor, WA: Logos Research Systems, Inc. 1997), 2Kings 2:1-10. CD-ROM (Logos Research System, Inc., 2002).

Chapter 4

1. James Swanson, *Dictionary of Biblical Languages with Semantic Domains: Greek (New Testament)* (Oak Harbor: Logos Research Systems, Inc., 1997).
2. Ibid.,72.
3. Alexander B. Bruce, *The Training of the Twelve* (Grand Rapids: Kregel Publications, 1992), 12.
4. Jesse Miranda, *Liderazgo y Amistad: Un Ministerio que Transforma* (Miami: Vida, 1998), 18.
5. Jan Johnson, *Spiritual Disciplines Companion: Bible Studies and Practices to Transform Your Soul* (Downers Grove: Intervarsity Press, 2009), 15.
6. Robert K. Greenleaf, *Servant Leadership: A Journey Into The Nature Of Legitimate Power And Greatness* (New York: Paulist Press, 1977), 14.

Chapter 5

1. Statistics of the Assemblies of God, "AG. Statistical Reports 2014," p. 2, AG. World Wide Churches p.2, http://agchurches.org/Sitefiles/Default/ RSS/AG.org%20TOP/AG%20Statistical%20Reports/2015%20 (year%202014%20reports)/2014%20Full%20Statistical%20Report. pdf (accessed January 12, 2016).
2. Assemblies of God, "Brief History of The Assemblies of God," front page, http://ag.org/top/about/History/index.cfm (accessed March 9, 2012).
3. Wayne L. Goodall, *By My Spirit: The Assemblies of God 1914-2000* (Springfield: Gospel Publishing House, 2000), 6.
4. Peter C. Wagner, *Your Spiritual Gifts Can Help Your Church Grow* (Ventura: Regal Books, 1994), 14.
5. Edith Waldvogel Blumhofer, *The Assemblies of God: A Popular History* (Springfield: Gospel Publishing House, 1985), 36.
6. Ibid., 37.
7. AG, "Statistical Reports 2014," 2,3,6,8.

8. Ibid., 3.
9. Bruce Rosdahl, "Whatever the Cost: The Formative Years of H. C. Ball, Pioneer of Hispanic Pentecostalism," *Journal of Assemblies of God Heritage* 31 (2001): 5-6.
10. Ibid.,5-11.
11. The complete name is Juanita Bazán, not to be confused with Nellie Bazán, Demetrio Bazán's wife.
12. Rosdahl, "Whatever the Cost," 6.
13. Ibid,. 7.
14. Rosdahl, "Whatever the Cost," 11.
15. Ibid,. 5.
16. David Bazán, interview by author, Burlingame, CA, March 16, 2012.
17. Nellie Bazán, *Enviados De Dios* (Miami: Editorial Vida, 1987), 16-29.
18. Victor De Leon, *The Silent Pentecostals: A Biographical History of the Pentecostal Movement Among the Hispanics in the Twentieth Century* (Taylors: Faith Printing Company, 1919), 95.
19. Ibid.
20. Bazán, *Enviados De Dios*, 54.
21. Bazán, *Enviados De Dios*, 108-123.
22. Ibid., 118.
23. Bazán, *Enviados De Dios*, 118.
24. Ibid., 180-184.

Chapter 6

1. Eldin Villafane, *The Liberating Spirit Toward an Hispanic American Pentecostal Social Ethic* (Grand Rapids: William B Eerdmans Publishing, 1993), 62.
2. Holland, *The Religious Dimension*, 191.
3. Ibid., 356.
4. Frank Bartleman, *Azusa Street* (Plainfield, NJ: Logos International, 1980), ix.
5. Holland, *The Religious Dimension*, 23.
6. De Leon, *The Silent Pentecostals*, 199.
7. Assemblies of God, *2014 Annual Report: Largest 100 U. S. AG Churches, as of December 31, 2014,* (Springfield: Assemblies of God, 2014), 1,2.
8. Nick Garza, phone interview by author, Sacramento, CA, January 13, 2016.

9   Statistics of the Assemblies of God, "AG. U.S. Ministers by District and Class, 2014," http://agchurches.org/Sitefiles/Default/RSS/AG.org%20TOP/AG%20Statistical%20Reports/2015%20 (year%202014%20reports)/Ide713%202014.pdf (accessed January 13, 2016) p. 1. Statistics of the Assemblies of God, "AG. U.S. Vital Statistics by Section, 2014," http://agchurches.org/Sitefiles/Default/RSS/AG.org%20TOP/AG%20Statistical%20Reports/2015%20 (year%202014%20reports)/Acm762%202014%20Sect%20Sum. pdf (accessed January 13, 2016) p.1. Statistics of the Assemblies of God, "AG. Ministers Age Summary 2014," http://agchurches. org/Sitefiles/Default/RSS/AG.org%20TOP/AG%20Statistical%20 Reports/2015%20%28year%202014%20reports%29/Sol766%20 2014%20Sum.pdf (accessed January 13, 2016) p. 201.

10.   Ibid., 6.

11.   Assemblies of God, *AG. Ministers Age Summary 2014*, 201.

12.   Northern Pacific Latin American District, *Constitution,* art. 2, sec. 1-2.

13.   Raul Sanchez, interview by author, Sacramento, CA, February 2, 2012.

Chapter 7

1 .   Miranda, *Liderazgo y Amistad*, 18, Translated from Spanish to English.

2 .   Miranda, 31.

Chapter 8

1.   Swanson, "Dictionary of Biblical Languages."

2.   Ibid.

3.   Clinton, *Leadership Emergence Theory*, 72.

4.   Alister E. McGrath, *Christian Spirituality: An Introduction* (Oxford: Blackwell, 1999), 2.

5.   Ralph Martin, *The Worship of God* (Michigan: William B. Eerdmans Publishing Company, 1982), 5.

6.   The New Unger's Bible Dictionary, "Worship" (Illinois: Moody Press of Chicago, 1988). CD-ROM (Logos Research System, Inc., 2002).

7 .   Ralph Martin, *Worship In The Early Church* (Grand Rapids: William B. Eerdmans Publishing House, 1964), 10.

8.   Martin, *The Worship of God,* 5.

9.   Everret Ferguson, "How Christians Worship," *Journal of Christian History* 37 (1998): 10-12.

10. Martin, *The Worship of God*, 17.
11. Richard J. Foster, *Prayer: Finding The Heart's True Home* (New York: HarperSanFrancisco, 1992).
12. St. Patrick, "The Breastplate of St. Patrick": translated from the Gaelic by Cecil Frances Humphreys Alexander, 1889. Jane Johnson, "Contemplative Spirituality" (Lecture, Azusa Pacific University, Azusa, CA, October 14, 2011).
13. Leo Grebler., Joan Moore., Ralph Guzman., et al. *The Mexican-American People: The Nation's Second Largest Minority* (New York: The Free Press, 1970), 296-297, 426-427, quoted by Clifton L. Holland, *The Religious Dimension In Hispanic Los Angeles: a Protestant Case Study* (South Pasadena: William Carey Library, 1974), 125.
14. Ibid.,125.
15. Assemblies of God, "2014 Annual Report: Largest 100 U. S. AG Churches," 1,2.
16. Holland, *The Religious Dimension*, 457.
17. Ortiz, *The Hispanic Challenge*, 128.
18. Jessica Martínez and Michael Lipka, "Hispanic Millennials are less religious than older U.S. Hispanics," *Journal of Pew Hispanic Center* (May 8, 2014): 1, http://www.pewresearch.org/fact-tank/2014/05/08/hispanic-millennials-are-less-religious-than-older-u-s-hispanics/ (Accessed April 26, 2016).
19. Robin Maas, Gabriel O'Donnell, O.P., eds., *Spiritual Traditions for the Contemporary Church* (Nashville: Abingdon, 1990), 18.

Chapter 9

1. Swanson, "Dictionary of Biblical Languages".
2. Keith Matthews, "Leadership Spirituality" (Lecture, Azusa Pacific University, Azusa, CA, January 5, 2010).
3. Dallas Willard, *The Great Omission* (Harper: San Francisco, 2006), xiv.
4. Dallas Willard, *The Divine Conspiracy: Rediscovering Our Hidden Life in God* (Harper: San Francisco, 1998), 41.
5. Dallas Willard, "Why Bother With Discipleship, I call it Heresy," *Journal of Renovare Perspective* 5, no. 6 (October 1995): 1, http://www.dwillard.org/articles/artview.asp?artID=71 (accessed June 22, 2012).

6. Dietrich Bonhoeffer, *The Cost of Discipleship*, quoted by John R. Tyson, *Invitation to Christian Spirituality: An ecumenical Anthology* (New York: Oxford University Press, 1999), 391,392.

7. Alexander Balmain Bruce, *The Training of the Twelve* (Grand Rapids: Kregel Publications, 1992) 39.

8. Clinton, *Leadership Emergence Theory,* 69.

9. Robert J. Clinton, *The Making of A Leader* (Colorado Springs: NavPress, 1988), 44.

10. Ibid.

11. Miranda, *Liderazgo y Amistad*, 31, Translated from Spanish to English.

12. For more information on texting and chat language, go to webopedia. com *Text Message Abbreviations* http://www.webopedia.com/quick_ref/textmessageabbreviations_02.asp (accessed March 15, 20012).

13. Holland, *The Religious Dimension*, 176.

14. David Kinnaman, "A Note from David Kinnaman," e-mail from author, December 7, 2011.

15. Robert Schuller, quoted from George Hunter III, *Church for the Unchurched* (Nashville: Abingdon, 1996), 71.

16. Dallas Willard, and Gary Black Jr. *The Divine Conspiracy Continued: Fulfilling God's Kingdom on Earth* (New York: Harper Collins, 2014), 31.

17. Eldin Villafañe, *The Liberating Spirit: Towards an Hispanic American Pentecostal Social Ethics* (Grand Rapids: William B. Eerdmans, 1993), 102.

18. Clinton, *Leadership Emergence Theory,* 74.

19. Merriam-Webster's Collegiate Dictionary. 11th ed. Springfield, MA: Merriam-Webster, 2003. "Experience."

20. Concise Oxford Dictionary of Literary Terms, 2d ed., s.v. "Experience."

21. James L. Garlow, *Partners in Ministry* (Kansas: Beacon Hill Press, 1981), 103.

22. Clinton, *Leadership Emergence Theory*, 432.

Chapter 10

1. Gene A. Getz, *Sharpening the Focus of the Church* (Chicago: Moody Press, 1974), 22.

2. Holland, *The Religious Dimension*, 457.

3. Ibid., 405.

4. John R. W. Stott, *Christian Mission in the Modern World* (Illinois: Intervarsity Press, 1975), 23.

5. Mary Douglas, *Purity and Danger: An analysis of the Concepts of Pollution and Taboo* (London: Routlegle, 1966), quoted by Miroslav Volf, *Exclusion & Embrace: A Theological Exploration of Identity, Otherness, and Reconciliation* (Nashville: Abingdon, 1996), 77-78.

6. Juan Gonzales, *Harvest of Empire: A History of Latinos in America* (New York: Penguin Group, 2000), 135-136.

7. Ibid., 138.

8. Leo R. Chavez, *Shadowed Lives: Undocumented Immigrants In American Society* (Wadsworth: Irvine, 1998), 40.

9. For information about the sb1070 see the following link: http://www.azleg.gov/legtext/49leg/2r/bills/sb1070s.pdf

10. Jens Manuel Krogstad, Ana Gonzalez-Barrera "Number of Latino children caught trying to enter U.S. nearly doubles in less than a year," *Journal of Pew Hispanic Center* (June 10, 2014): 1, http://www.pewresearch.org/fact-tank/2014/06/10/number-of-latino-children-caught-trying-to-enter-u-s-nearly-doubles-in-less-than-a-year/ (accessed April 25, 2016).

11. Glen H. Stassen, David P. Gushee, *Kingdom Ethics: Following Jesus In Contemporary Context* (Illinois: Inter Varsity Press, 2003) 39.

12. Willard and Black Jr., *The Divine Conspiracy Continued*, 105.

13. G. Frank, "U.S. Baja Officials to act on Border Strife," Los Angeles Times, Sec. 2, p. 161. Quoted by Leo R. Chavez, *Shadowed Lives: Undocumented Immigrants In American Society* (Wadsworth: Irvine, 1998), 61.

14. Walter Wink, *Engaging The Powers: Discernment and Resistance in a World of Domination* (Minneapolis: Augsburg Fortress, 1992), 263.

15. Monica McGoldrick, Kenneth V. Hardy, *Re-Visioning Family Therapy* (New York: The Guilford Press, 2008), 25.

16. Manz, Beatriz, Perry-Houts, Ingrid, Castaneda, Xochitl. "Guatemalan Immigration to the San Francisco Area," *Center for Latino Policy Research, UC Berkeley*, September 09, 2000. http://escholarship.org/uc/item/6t20159p?pageNum=10# (accessed March 31, 2012).

17. Daryl Arnold, Jerry Brown, Cesar Chavez, "The Fight in the Fields: Cesar Chavez and The Farmworkers' Struggle," DVD-ROM (Cinema Guild, 2007).

18. Bryant L. Myers, *Walking With The Poor* (New York: Orbis Books, 1999), 35.

19. Ibid., 71.

Chapter 11

1. Fred R. Shapiro, "John A. Shedd," *The Yale Book of Quotations* (New Haven: Yale University Press, 2006), Page 705. Quoted by Garson O'Toole, "A Ship in Harbor Is Safe, But that Is Not What Ships Are Built For," Garson O'Toole Blog, entry posted (December 09, 2013): 1. http://quoteinvestigator.com/2013/12/09/safe-harbor/ (accessed on March 24,2016)
2. Sanchez, interview by author, Sacramento, CA, February 2, 2012.
3. Clinton, *Leadership Emergence Theory*, 186.
4. J. Robert Clinton and Paul D. Stanley., eds., *Connecting: The Mentoring Relationship You Need to Succeed In Life*. Colorado Springs: NavPress, 1992), 24-25.
5. Sam Farina, "Coaching Next-Generation Leaders," *Journal of Enrichment* 17, no. 2 (Spring 2012): 79.
6. Ibid., 79.
7. NPLAD, "Influence With Impact Manual," 1.
8. Holland, *The Religious Dimension*, 468.
9. Brian Raison as quoted by Jeff Schadt "Going Going Gone: Protecting Teens' Hearts That Are On The Edge" http://ytn.org/documents/ GoingGoingGoneExcerpts.pdf 2. (accessed on June 8, 2012).
10. Eddie Gibbs, *Church Next:Quantum Changes in How We Do Ministry* (Downers Grove: Intervarsity Press, 2000) 93.
11. Goodall, *By My Spirit*, 9-10.

About the Author

D r. **Maynor Morales** is an ordained minister of the Assemblies of God. He served as a senior pastor of a bilingual church at New Dawn Worship Center/Centro de Adoración Nuevo Amanecer in Fremont California for over fifteen years. He also served as a director of evangelism and executive presbyter at a Hispanic district of the Assemblies of God. In the area of Christian education, he has been teaching courses on Biblical studies and theology since 1994. He was a director of the Latin American Bible Institute (LABI), Extension Fremont, from 2002-2013, and of the Latin American Theological Seminary (LATS), Extension Fremont, from 2007-2013.

Dr. Morales's father (Matias Morales) was a church planter, pastor, and missionary for over seventy-five years. It was his father's mentorship and legacy that paved the way for Dr. Morales's passion for evangelism, leadership development and empowering the emerging generation. Maynor's desire to see new converts and more disciples into God's kingdom is the main reason for his travels around the world for the last thirty-seven years, holding evangelistic crusades, conferences, and seminars. He is an associate member and professor of a ministry called Ministerio Internacional Vision Misionera (International Ministry Vision Missionary) led by Rev. Enoc Paredes, whose primary goal is to train pastors and laypeople for leadership, by opening Bible institutes and leadership centers for Latinos in Asia, Australia, and Europe.

A few years ago and after obtaining his Doctor of Ministry degree from Azusa Pacific University, Dr. Morales, alongside his wife Evelyn, (author of the book *Discover the True Wonder Woman in You*) and their two daughters, Krystal and Tiffany, answered a call from the Lord to plant a church in Fort Worth Texas, where they currently reside.

For **speaking engagements** you may contact Dr. Morales at **moralestx1@gmail.com or via Facebook at www.facebook. com/drmaynor.morales** You can also write to him at P.O. Box 136761, Lake Worth, TX, 76136.

If this book has been a blessing to you, share the message by doing the following:

- Pick up a copy and bless your leader, pastor, teacher or a member of the Emerging Hispanic Generation.
- Recommend it to Christian educational entities for their consideration.
- Consider using it as a manual for studies related to this topic amongst small groups, or fellowship groups.
- Share it on social media, or write a book review online.
- Write to us and let us know if it has been helpful in any way.
- Contact Dr. Maynor Morales for a speaking engagement (evangelistic crusades, teaching Bible courses or seminars on leadership).
- Pray for us and our ministry. Our desire is to be a blessing and to share the gospel with anyone, anywhere, at any cost.

Printed in the USA
CPSIA information can be obtained
at www.ICGtesting.com
JSHW010311250124
55699JS00010B/124